"Angus Chu's book superbly manages to teach undergraduate students the intertemporal macroeconomic methods needed to fully understand the research going on in this field. Hence it fills an important gap in the current didactic literature, which badly misses it and leaves Bachelor students unable to write, for example, a theoretical thesis. Without dwelling on abstract math, this book introduces intertemporal methods directly into the most important macroeconomics topics, spanning from the neoclassical workhorse growth and business cycle framework to the basic New Keynesian model to recent R&D-driven growth theory. I strongly recommend this book in any good economics curriculum."

Professor Guido Cozzi
University of St. Gallen, Switzerland

"Angus Chu's text is an excellent exposition of modern macroeconomics for advanced undergraduates, filling a gap between intermediate and advanced graduate material. It is distinctive as it systematically develops models from first principles using dynamic optimisation techniques. Macroeconomics involves studying variables over time and this concise and lucid book introduces the framework of modern macroeconomics. It shows the development of ideas and to go from studying growth, to business cycles, to monetary and fiscal policy with the same framework and tools."

Professor Aditya Goenka
University of Birmingham, UK

"The book introduces the tools of modern dynamic macroeconomics to an advanced undergraduate audience in a user-friendly way. It fills the gap between the standard undergraduate textbook with very little or no calculus and the graduate textbook with too much mathematics for an undergraduate course. The presentation of modern growth theory is excellent, allowing readers to access frontier tools and research topics at a fairly low technical cost. I envision this book being a useful tool in the classroom."

Professor Giammario Impullitti
University of Nottingham, UK

"This book provides an excellent overview of the key macroeconomic models with relevance for government policy. In doing so, it addresses not only the traditional models, but it also gives insights from recent research in this field. The book is a useful toolkit for those who wish to go beyond the standard macroeconomic models; it provides various roadmaps to tackle challenging modern policy questions."

Professor Jozef Konings
The University of Liverpool, UK

"This is a highly readable and easily accessible account of the modern tools and practices in macroeconomic theory and policy in the context of both developed and emerging market economies. It is essential reading for those with an interest in the issues of alternative approaches in policy modelling. This advanced textbook offers an interesting blend of analytical, quantitative and policy insights about the best means to model and assess different mechanisms of economic growth and macroeconomic policy questions."

Professor Sushanta Mallick
Queen Mary University of London, UK

"Angus Chu covers the dynamic general-equilibrium approach to macroeconomics in a way that is accessible to advanced undergraduate students. This approach has the potential to change the way undergraduate students think about modern macroeconomics. This book covers a range of policy issues, such as fiscal policy, monetary policy, and innovation policy, in a coherent analytical framework, which has the advantage of helping students understand how different topics in macroeconomics relate to each other."

Professor Pietro Peretto
Duke University, USA

"An excellent textbook that covers a substantial number of advanced macroeconomic topics. This is a wonderful learning and reference guide designed for undergraduate students who want to explore advanced macroeconomics and can be easily adopted at postgraduate level. The textbook presents modern macroeconomic views via a selection of neoclassical and New Keynesian

models. Concepts such as profit maximisation, general equilibrium, consumption, labour, capital and money supply are carefully explained. The theoretical insights are accompanied by fiscal and monetary policies analysis. The book also covers a wealth of economic growth models including different market structures and endogenous technological change. This stimulating book provides students with solid grounding and rigorous analysis of mathematical modelling. I particularly like the easy-to-follow structure and comprehensive language which are unique features possessed by this must-have book."

Professor Oleksandr Talavera
University of Birmingham, UK

"Filling the gap between undergraduate and graduate textbooks has always been a challenge. Using Advanced Macroeconomics: An Introduction for Undergraduates, *instructors can meet it. This well written textbook expertly bridges the gap between the two levels of study. The author starts with the one sector growth model, the workhorse model of modern macroeconomics. He extends this model in several directions in one step at the time to make the material easily accessible for students. In this way, students get well acquainted with the basic toolkit of modern macroeconomics, and the rigorous policy analysis shows them how and when the government can improve upon market outcomes."*

Professor Akos Valentinyi
University of Manchester, UK

ADVANCED MACRO-ECONOMICS

An Introduction for
Undergraduates

ADVANCED MACRO-ECONOMICS
An Introduction for
Undergraduates

Angus C. Chu
University of Liverpool, UK

Foreword by **Guido Cozzi**

With contributions from **Xilin Wang**

 **World Scientific**

NEW JERSEY · LONDON · SINGAPORE · BEIJING · SHANGHAI · HONG KONG · TAIPEI · CHENNAI · TOKYO

Published by

World Scientific Publishing Europe Ltd.

57 Shelton Street, Covent Garden, London WC2H 9HE

Head office: 5 Toh Tuck Link, Singapore 596224

USA office: 27 Warren Street, Suite 401-402, Hackensack, NJ 07601

Library of Congress Cataloging-in-Publication Data

Names: Chu, Angus C., 1978–   author.

Title: Advanced macroeconomics : an introduction for undergraduates /
    Angus C. Chu, University of Liverpool, UK ; with contributions from Xilin Wang.

Description: USA : World Scientific, 2020. | Includes bibliographical references and index.

Identifiers: LCCN 2020037076 | ISBN 9781786349125 (hardcover) |
    ISBN 9781786349132 (ebook) | ISBN 9781786349149 (ebook other)

Subjects: LCSH: Macroeconomics.

Classification: LCC HB172.5 .C478 2020 | DDC 339--dc23

LC record available at https://lccn.loc.gov/2020037076

British Library Cataloguing-in-Publication Data

A catalogue record for this book is available from the British Library.

For any available supplementary material, please visit
https://www.worldscientific.com/worldscibooks/10.1142/Q0267#t=suppl

Desk Editors: Aanand Jayaraman/Michael Beale/Shi Ying Koe

Typeset by Stallion Press
Email: enquiries@stallionpress.com

Printed in Singapore

In memory of Elsie

Foreword

Undergraduate students often find macroeconomics frustrating. Many books they encounter in their career explain the main theories in good detail, while surgically avoiding teaching the underlying intertemporal methods. This widespread approach leaves the students of macroeconomics in a disturbingly unclear state of mind. They suspect that there is something more rigorous behind the simple graphs they are shown but also realise that they cannot fully understand what it really is.

Angus Chu's *Advanced Macroeconomics* does quite the opposite: it follows a rigorous and crystal clear path from start to finish. During this process, students will gradually build up the analytical skills to eventually help them find their way through the highly complex frontier of research in macroeconomics. I am sure that they will appreciate this effort and be grateful to its author.

Personally, I would not have expected anything less rigorous from a macroeconomic theory master like Angus Chu. Since I met him, many years ago, in a dinner at Shanghai, where half an hour of creative discussion about a potential new theory ended up in some twenty hand-written pages of perfectly consistent mathematical formulas, I know Angus would never deliver any half-explained or half-analysed theory. In a book for undergraduate students, he would rather simplify the ornaments of some theories while keeping the focus at the highest analytical standard. This is exactly what is needed to build a sound bridge between bachelor and post-graduate studies. Equipped with a careful study of this book, students will be able to successfully start their theses without too much fear of reading the frontier literature. It will also avoid the scenario of students graduating and then becoming traumatised by the mathematics they suddenly see in their first months of their Master or PhD classes.

In studying this book, the reader will receive a complete training in macroeconomics, highlighting all the most important concepts and accompanying the student through the build-up of necessary methodologies. At the same time, this book, in the style of the author, will not be a nasty trainer but rather a gentle, gradual reinforcement of the reader's skills. Concepts are introduced in a very digestible sequence, without putting too much burden on the learning process. Hence I think that students with one or two years of standard economics studies will relatively easily manage to digest and understand this book. With all that in mind, I wish the reader enjoys reading this book as much as I have.

Professor Guido Cozzi
University of St. Gallen, Switzerland

Preface

This book covers selected topics in advanced macroeconomics at the undergraduate level and bridges the gap between intermediate macroeconomics for undergraduates and advanced macroeconomics for postgraduates. By building on materials in intermediate macroeconomics textbooks (e.g., Barro *et al.*, 2017) and covering the mathematics of some classic dynamic general-equilibrium models, this book will give undergraduate students a firm appreciation of modern developments in macroeconomics.

Dynamic general equilibrium is the foundation of modern macroeconomics. Chapter 1 begins with a simple static model to demonstrate the concept of general equilibrium. Chapters 2–4 cover the neoclassical growth model to explore the effects of exogenous changes in the level of technology, which are an important source of business cycle fluctuations. Chapters 5–7 use the neoclassical growth model to explore the effects of fiscal policy instruments, such as government spending, labour income tax and capital income tax. Chapter 8 develops a simple New Keynesian model to analyse the effects of monetary policy.

Chapter 9 begins the analysis of economic growth by reviewing the Solow growth model. Chapters 10–12 present the Ramsey model and introduce different market structures to the model to lay down the foundation of the Romer model. Chapter 13 incorporates an R&D sector into the Ramsey model with a monopolistically competitive market structure to develop the Romer model of endogenous technological change. Chapters 14 and 15 examine the implications of the Romer model. Chapter 16 concludes this book by presenting the Schumpeterian growth model and examining its different implications from the Romer model.

About the Author

 **Angus C. Chu** was born in Hong Kong and studied at Simon Fraser University and the University of British Columbia in Canada. He obtained his PhD degree in Economics from the University of Michigan in the US. He is currently Chair in Macroeconomics at the University of Liverpool in the UK and was previously Professor of Economics at Fudan University in China. Angus's research focuses on macroeconomics, monetary economics, economic growth, innovation and intellectual property rights. His research appears in journals, such as the *European Economic Review, International Economic Review, Journal of Development Economics, Journal of Economic Growth, Journal of International Economics, Journal of Money, Credit and Banking*, and the *Review of Economic Dynamics*. His textbook *Intermediate Macroeconomics* with Robert J. Barro and Guido Cozzi was published by Cengage Learning in 2017. According to IDEAS/RePEc Rankings, he is among the top 10% of economists in the world. He also serves as a Co-Editor-in-Chief for *Economic Modelling*.

Acknowledgements

My biggest debt is to Amanda, Alvin and Alice for their loving support. I am also very grateful for the helpful comments and feedback from my students at Fudan University and the University of Liverpool.

Contents

Chapter 1

A Static General-Equilibrium Model

Dynamic general equilibrium is the foundation of modern macroeconomic models. In this chapter, we first explore the concept of general equilibrium using a simple static model. Our simple economy involves two groups of economic agents: consumers and firms. We consider a representative household, which determines the behaviour of consumers. We also consider a representative firm, which determines the behaviour of firms. The representative household supplies labour and capital to the representative firm, which then uses these factor inputs to produce output and sells the output back to the household. We use this model to explore how changes in the level of technology affect the labour market and the capital market and how the two markets interact with each other.

1.1. The Model

In general, the representative household maximises utility. For now, we simply assume that the household supplies labour L^s and capital K^s inelastically to earn a wage income W and a capital rental income R. Perfectly inelastic supply implies a vertical labour supply curve (i.e., $L^s = \overline{L}$) and a vertical capital supply curve ($K^s = \overline{K}$), where $\overline{L}$ and $\overline{K}$ are exogenous parameters.

We now consider the firm's optimisation problem. The representative firm hires labour L and rents capital K from the household to produce output Y using the following Cobb–Douglas production function:

$$Y = AK^\alpha L^{1-\alpha}, \tag{1.1}$$

where the parameter $\alpha \in (0,1)$ is the degree of capital intensity in production and A is the exogenous level of technology. The profit function Π is

$$\Pi = PY - RK - WL. \tag{1.2}$$

We consider a perfectly competitive product market, in which the firm takes the market price P as given.

To maximise profit, we differentiate (1.2) with respect to K and L:

$$\frac{\partial \Pi}{\partial K} = P\frac{\partial Y}{\partial K} - R = 0, \tag{1.3}$$

$$\frac{\partial \Pi}{\partial L} = P\frac{\partial Y}{\partial L} - W = 0. \tag{1.4}$$

Rewriting (1.3) and (1.4) yields

$$\frac{\partial Y}{\partial K} = \alpha AK^{\alpha-1}L^{1-\alpha} = \frac{R}{P}, \tag{1.5}$$

$$\frac{\partial Y}{\partial L} = (1-\alpha)AK^\alpha L^{-\alpha} = \frac{W}{P}, \tag{1.6}$$

which states that a profit-maximising firm would equate the marginal product of capital to the real rental price R/P and the marginal product of labour to the real wage rate W/P.

Equations (1.5) and (1.6) are the demand curves for capital and labour. To see this, they can be re-expressed as

$$K^d = \left(\frac{\alpha A}{R/P}\right)^{1/(1-\alpha)} L, \tag{1.7}$$

$$L^d = \left[\frac{(1-\alpha)A}{W/P}\right]^{1/\alpha} K, \tag{1.8}$$

where capital demand K^d is decreasing in the real rental price R/P and labour demand L^d is decreasing in the real wage rate W/P. In other words, the demand for capital and labour is determined by the profit-maximising behaviour of firms. We also have the following implications from (1.7) and (1.8). First, an increase in the level of technology increases the demand for capital and labour. Second, an increase in the level of labour increases the demand for capital. Third, an increase in the level of capital increases the demand for labour.

1.2. Equilibrium

Combining the demand and supply curves of capital (labour) yields the equilibrium level of the real rental price (real wage rate) as follows:

$$\frac{R}{P} = \alpha A \left(\frac{\overline{L}}{\overline{K}}\right)^{1-\alpha}, \tag{1.9}$$

$$\frac{W}{P} = (1 - \alpha)A \left(\frac{\overline{K}}{\overline{L}}\right)^{\alpha}. \tag{1.10}$$

Together with the production function

$$Y = A\overline{K}^{\alpha}\overline{L}^{1-\alpha}, \tag{1.11}$$

we have the following results. First, an increase in the level of technology A raises the level of output Y, the real rental price R/P (by increasing capital demand) and the real wage rate W/P (by increasing labour demand); see Figures 1.1 and 1.2.

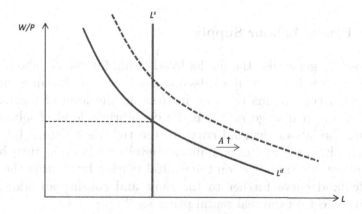

Figure 1.1. Labour market: Inelastic labour supply.

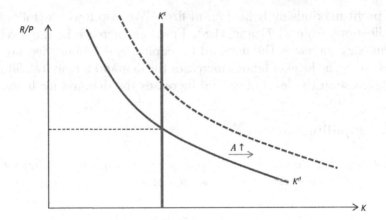

Figure 1.2.   Capital market: Inelastic capital supply.

Second, an increase in the level of capital $\overline{K}$ increases the level of output Y and the real wage rate W/P but decreases the real rental price R/P. Third, an increase in the level of labour $\overline{L}$ increases the level of output Y and the real rental price R/P but decreases the real wage rate W/P. As we can see, changes in the supply of one factor input (e.g., labour) not only affect its own market (e.g., labour market) but also affect the other market (e.g., capital market). This interaction between the two markets represents a *general-equilibrium* effect.

1.3.   Elastic Labour Supply

Suppose we generalise the model by allowing for elastic labour supply. Then we have an upward-sloping labour supply curve in the labour market. In this case, an increase in the level of technology A raises the real wage rate and the equilibrium level of labour by shifting the labour demand curve to the right; see Figure 1.3. The resulting increase in the equilibrium level of labour in turn has a general-equilibrium effect on the capital market by shifting the capital demand curve further to the right and causing an additional positive effect on the real rental price; see Figure 1.4.

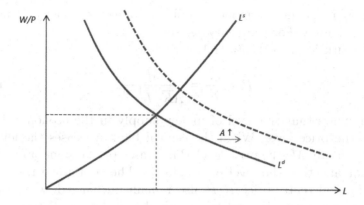

Figure 1.3.   Labour market: Elastic labour supply.

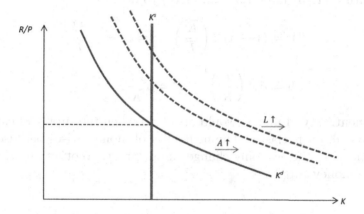

Figure 1.4.   Capital market: Elastic labour supply.

1.4.   Neutrality of Money

So far, we have only determined the real wage rate W/P and the real rental price R/P. However, we haven't determined the nominal wage rate W and the nominal rental price R, which in turn are determined by the price level P. To determine the price level, we introduce the quantity theory of money:

$$MV = PY, \tag{1.12}$$

where M is the level of money supply and V is the velocity of money in the economy. For simplicity, we set $V = 1$.[1]

Substituting (1.11) into (1.12), we have

$$P = \frac{M}{Y} = \frac{M}{A\overline{K}^{\alpha}\overline{L}^{1-\alpha}}, \tag{1.13}$$

which shows that the level of money supply in the economy determines the price level. When the central bank increases the level of money supply M, the price level P increases by the same proportion without affecting the level of output Y. The real wage rate W/P and the real rental price R/P also remain unchanged, whereas the nominal wage rate W and the nominal rental price R increase by the same proportion as the level of money supply M. To see this, we substitute (1.13) into (1.9) and (1.10) to derive

$$W = (1-\alpha)A\left(\frac{\overline{K}}{\overline{L}}\right)^{\alpha} P = (1-\alpha)\frac{M}{\overline{L}}, \tag{1.14}$$

$$R = \alpha A\left(\frac{\overline{L}}{\overline{K}}\right)^{1-\alpha} P = \alpha\frac{M}{\overline{K}}. \tag{1.15}$$

This neutrality of money would also hold when the supply of capital and/or labour is elastic. The neutrality of money arises because the price level in the economy changes immediately to offset any change in the money supply.[2]

1.5. Summary

In this chapter, we use a simple static general-equilibrium model to explore the effects of technology on the economy. We find that an increase in the level of technology raises the level of output, the real rental price and the real wage rate. In the case of elastic labour supply, the equilibrium level of labour also increases, which in turn has a general-equilibrium effect on the capital market by shifting the capital demand curve further to the right and causing a larger

---

[1]Our analysis would hold so long as the money velocity V is exogenous.

[2]In Chapter 8, we will consider a New Keynesian model in which the neutrality of money does not hold because prices do not adjust immediately.

increase in the real rental price. We also explore the effects of changes in the level of money supply and find that money supply only affects nominal variables (i.e., the price level, the nominal rental price and the nominal wage rate) without affecting any of the real variables (i.e., the level of output, the real rental price, the real wage rate, the level of labour and the level of capital). This result is known as the classical dichotomy, according to which real and nominal variables can be determined separately.

1.6. Exercises

1. How do changes in the level of technology affect the labour and capital markets when both labour supply and capital supply are elastic?
2. Show that the neutrality of money holds when the supply of capital and/or labour is elastic.
3. Suppose the supply of capital is elastic. How does an increase in the supply of labour affect the nominal variables?
4. Suppose the supply of labour is chosen by a utility-maximising household with the following utility function:

$$U = C - \frac{\beta L^2}{2},$$

where β determines the importance of leisure relative to consumption C. The household's budget constraint is given by

$$PC \le WL + RK.$$

Show that the labour supply function L^s is given by

$$L^s = \frac{1}{\beta} \frac{W}{P},$$

which is increasing in the real wage rate W/P.

5. How do changes in β in Exercise 4 affect the labour and capital markets when capital supply is perfectly inelastic (i.e., $K = \overline{K}$)?
6. How do changes in β in Exercise 4 affect the labour and capital markets when capital supply is elastic?

Chapter 2

The Neoclassical Growth Model

In this chapter, we convert the static general-equilibrium model into a dynamic general-equilibrium model, which is the foundation of modern macroeconomics. Specifically, we consider the neoclassical growth model, in which the representative household chooses consumption and saving to maximise lifetime utility. To solve this dynamic optimisation problem, we use a mathematical tool known as the Hamiltonian.[1] This analysis enables us to endogenise the equilibrium levels of macroeconomic variables, such as capital and output, in order to explore their determinants, such as the level of technology and the preference of the representative household.

2.1. Household

In the neoclassical growth model, there is a representative household, which has a utility function u_t at time t. For simplicity, we consider a log utility function $u_t = \ln C_t$ that depends on consumption C_t. In other words, increasing consumption makes the household better off. Furthermore, the log utility function has a number of nice properties. For example, it features diminishing marginal utility, and the log

---

[1]In intermediate microeconomics, students often use the Lagrangian for solving static constrained optimisation problems. In the case of dynamic optimisation problems, we use the Hamiltonian instead.

of zero is negative infinity so that the household would avoid zero consumption.

A forward-looking household should not only care about utility at time t but also lifetime utility, which is given by

$$U = u_0 + u_1 + u_2 + \cdots = \sum_{t=0}^{T} u_t, \tag{2.1}$$

where T is the length of a lifetime. Equation (2.1) assumes that current utility and future utility carry the same weight, which is unrealistic because future consumption is often discounted. To capture discounting, we introduce a discount rate $\rho > 0$ so that (2.1) becomes

$$U = u_0 + \frac{u_1}{1 + \rho} + \frac{u_2}{(1 + \rho)^2} + \cdots = \sum_{t=0}^{\infty} \frac{u_t}{(1 + \rho)^t}, \tag{2.2}$$

where we assume that a lifetime is long enough to be approximated by infinity.[2] In the rest of the analysis, we will use a mathematical tool known as Hamiltonian that solves dynamic optimisation problems in continuous time. Therefore, we need to rewrite (2.2) in continuous time using the integral as

$$U = \int_{0}^{\infty} e^{-\rho t} u_t dt = \int_{0}^{\infty} e^{-\rho t} \ln C_t dt, \tag{2.3}$$

where the continuous-time discount factor $e^{-\rho t}$ replaces the discrete-time discount factor $(1 + \rho)^{-t}$.

The household inelastically supplies L units of labour to earn a wage income W_t. Furthermore, it accumulates capital K_t and rents it to the representative firm to earn a capital-rental income R_t. We assume that capital is the only productive asset in the economy.[3] If we

---

[2] As t becomes very large, the discounting would make $u_t/(1+\rho)^t$ not to matter too much in the utility function U.

[3] Introducing a bond that is in zero net supply would allow us to determine the real interest rate but would not affect the rest of our analysis.

normalise the price of output to unity,[4] then the asset-accumulation equation is[5]

$$\dot{K}_t = R_t K_t + W_t L - C_t, \tag{2.4}$$

where $\dot{K}_t \equiv \partial K_t / \partial t$ is the change in the level of capital with respect to time t. Here we have assumed a zero depreciation rate of capital (i.e., $\delta = 0$).[6]

2.2. Hamiltonian

The household maximises (2.3) subject to (2.4). To solve this dynamic optimisation problem, we use the Hamiltonian.[7] The Hamiltonian function H_t is given by

$$H_t = \ln C_t + \lambda_t (R_t K_t + W_t L - C_t). \tag{2.5}$$

In other words, the Hamiltonian function at time t consists of (a) the utility function $\ln C_t$, (b) the right-hand side of the asset-accumulation equation $R_t K_t + W_t L - C_t$, and (c) a multiplier λ_t for the asset-accumulation equation.

To maximise the household's utility, we derive the first-order conditions, which include

$$\frac{\partial H_t}{\partial C_t} = \frac{1}{C_t} - \lambda_t = 0, \tag{2.6}$$

$$\frac{\partial H_t}{\partial K_t} = \lambda_t R_t = \lambda_t \rho - \dot{\lambda}_t. \tag{2.7}$$

Note that K_t is a state variable (i.e., a variable that accumulates over time), so we have to treat its first-order condition differently.

---

[4]Recall from Chapter 1 that money supply determines the price level without affecting any of the real variables in the economy.

[5]Here we assume that one unit of output can be converted into one unit of consumption or one unit of capital.

[6]In general, the asset-accumulation equation is given by $\dot{K}_t = (R_t - \delta)K_t + W_t L - C_t$.

[7]See the appendix on dynamic optimisation for further details.

Instead of equating $\partial H_t / \partial K_t$ to zero, we set $\partial H_t / \partial K_t = \lambda_t \rho - \dot{\lambda}_t$. Taking the log of (2.6) yields

$$\ln C_t = -\ln \lambda_t. \qquad (2.8)$$

Differentiating both sides of (2.8) with respect to t yields[8]

$$\frac{\dot{C}_t}{C_t} = -\frac{\dot{\lambda}_t}{\lambda_t}. \qquad (2.9)$$

Substituting this equation into (2.7) yields

$$\frac{\dot{C}_t}{C_t} = -\frac{\dot{\lambda}_t}{\lambda_t} = R_t - \rho, \qquad (2.10)$$

which is the optimal path of consumption chosen by the household.

The optimal consumption path in (2.10) states that when the rental price R_t is greater than the discount rate ρ, the household's consumption should be increasing over time (i.e., $\dot{C}_t > 0$). Intuitively, when the return to capital is high relative to the household's discount rate, the household should decrease current consumption and increase saving in order to invest in capital. As a result, consumption is increasing over time. Conversely, when the rental price R_t is less than the discount rate ρ, the household's consumption should be decreasing over time (i.e., $\dot{C}_t < 0$). Intuitively, when the return to capital is low relative to the household's discount rate, the household should increase current consumption and decrease investment in capital. As a result, consumption is decreasing over time.

2.3. Firm

To derive the equilibrium of the economy, we also need to consider the firm's optimisation problem, which is quite simple because of its static setting. There is a representative firm in the economy, and this firm hires labour L_t and rents capital K_t from the household to produce output Y_t using the following Cobb–Douglas production

---

[8]Note that $\frac{\partial \ln C_t}{\partial t} = \frac{1}{C_t} \frac{\partial C_t}{\partial t} = \frac{\dot{C}_t}{C_t}$.

function:

$$Y_t = AK_t^\alpha L_t^{1-\alpha}, \tag{2.11}$$

where the parameter $\alpha \in (0,1)$ is the degree of capital intensity in production and A is the exogenous level of technology. The profit function Π_t is

$$\Pi_t = Y_t - R_t K_t - W_t L_t. \tag{2.12}$$

Recall that we have chosen Y_t as the numeraire (i.e., the price of Y_t is normalised to unity). Differentiating (2.12) with respect to K_t and L_t yields

$$\frac{\partial \Pi_t}{\partial K_t} = \frac{\partial Y_t}{\partial K_t} - R_t = \alpha A K_t^{\alpha-1} L_t^{1-\alpha} - R_t = 0, \tag{2.13}$$

$$\frac{\partial \Pi_t}{\partial L_t} = \frac{\partial Y_t}{\partial L_t} - W_t = (1-\alpha)A K_t^\alpha L_t^{-\alpha} - W_t = 0. \tag{2.14}$$

These two equations are the demand functions for K_t and L_t.

2.4. Steady-State Equilibrium

Substituting $R_t = \alpha A K_t^{\alpha-1} L_t^{1-\alpha}$ from (2.13) into (2.10) yields

$$\frac{\dot{C}_t}{C_t} = \underbrace{\alpha A K_t^{\alpha-1} L^{1-\alpha}}_{=MPK_t} - \rho, \tag{2.15}$$

where we have set $L_t = L$. Equation (2.15) shows that the optimal path of consumption is determined by the return to capital, which in turn is determined by the marginal product of capital MPK_t. Substituting $R_t = \alpha A K_t^{\alpha-1} L^{1-\alpha}$ and $W_t = (1-\alpha)A K_t^\alpha L^{-\alpha}$ from (2.13) and (2.14) into (2.4) yields the capital-accumulation equation:

$$\dot{K}_t = \alpha A K_t^\alpha L^{1-\alpha} + (1-\alpha)A K_t^\alpha L^{1-\alpha} - C_t = A K_t^\alpha L^{1-\alpha} - C_t. \tag{2.16}$$

This equation shows that the accumulation of capital is determined by capital investment, which is the difference between output and consumption. Equations (2.15) and (2.16) are two differential equations in C_t and K_t, and these two equations determine the behaviour of the economy.

Now we solve for the steady-state equilibrium.[9] In the steady state, all variables are constant, such that $\dot{C}_t = 0$ and $\dot{K}_t = 0$. Imposing $\dot{C}_t = 0$ on the optimal consumption path in (2.15) yields the steady-state equilibrium level of capital:

$$K^* = \left(\frac{\alpha A}{\rho}\right)^{1/(1-\alpha)} L, \qquad (2.17)$$

which is increasing in the level of technology A and decreasing in the discount rate ρ. Intuitively, a higher level of technology A increases the return to capital and encourages the household to accumulate more capital. In contrast, a higher discount rate makes future consumption less attractive to the household, which prefers current consumption and accumulates less capital.

Equation (2.17) also allows us to quantify the effects on K^*. For example, the elasticity of K^* with respect to A is $1/(1 - \alpha)$. To see this, $\partial \ln K^*/\partial \ln A = 1/(1 - \alpha)$.[10] In other words, increasing technology A by 1% would lead to an increase in capital K^* by $1/(1-\alpha)$ percent. If $\alpha = 1/3$, then $1/(1-\alpha)$ is 1.5. If $\alpha = 1/2$, then $1/(1 - \alpha)$ is 2.

Using the production function in (2.11), we can derive the steady-state equilibrium level of output:

$$Y^* = A(K^*)^\alpha L^{1-\alpha} = \left(\frac{\alpha A}{\rho}\right)^{\alpha/(1-\alpha)} AL, \qquad (2.18)$$

which is increasing in A via a direct effect from A on Y and an indirect effect from A on K^*. The elasticity of Y^* with respect to A is also $1/(1-\alpha)$.[11] Steady-state output Y^* is decreasing in ρ because a smaller capital stock K^* reduces the level of output Y^*.

---

[9]One can use the phase diagram of (2.15) and (2.16) to show that the economy converges to this steady state.

[10]Note that $\frac{d \ln K^*}{d \ln A} = \frac{dK^*}{K^*}/\frac{dA}{A}$, which is the elasticity of K^* with respect to A.

[11]Note that $1 + \alpha/(1 - \alpha) = 1/(1 - \alpha)$.

Imposing $\dot{K}_t = 0$ on the capital-accumulation equation in (2.16) yields the steady-state equilibrium level of consumption:

$$C^* = A(K^*)^\alpha L^{1-\alpha} = \left(\frac{\alpha A}{\rho}\right)^{\alpha/(1-\alpha)} AL, \qquad (2.19)$$

which is also increasing in A and decreasing in ρ because $C^* = Y^*$. In this special case of $\delta = 0$, the steady-state equilibrium level of investment is $I^* = Y^* - C^* = 0$. However, in the more general case of $\delta > 0$, the steady-state equilibrium level of investment would be positive; see Exercise 1 at the end of this chapter.

2.5. Summary

In this chapter, we explore the concept of dynamic general equilibrium by developing the neoclassical growth model. The model features a utility-maximising representative household, which chooses consumption and saving optimally. We use the Hamiltonian to solve this dynamic optimisation problem and derive the household's optimal consumption path, in which the growth rate of consumption is increasing in the rental price of capital and decreasing in the household's discount rate. A profit-maximising representative firm interacts with the utility-maximising household in the market economy that determines the allocation of resources in equilibrium. Then, we derive the steady-state equilibrium levels of capital and output, which are both increasing in the level of technology but decreasing in the household's discount rate and also the depreciation rate of capital (see Exercise 1).

2.6. Exercises

1. Consider a positive capital depreciation rate $\delta > 0$. In this case, the asset-accumulation equation becomes

$$\dot{K}_t = (R_t - \delta)K_t + W_t L - C_t. \qquad (2.20)$$

Show that the optimal consumption path is given by

$$\frac{\dot{C}_t}{C_t} = R_t - \delta - \rho \qquad (2.21)$$

and that the steady-state equilibrium levels of $\{K^*, Y^*, I^*, C^*\}$ are given by

$$K^* = \left(\frac{\alpha A}{\rho + \delta}\right)^{1/(1-\alpha)} L, \tag{2.22}$$

$$Y^* = A(K^*)^\alpha L^{1-\alpha} = \left(\frac{\alpha A}{\rho + \delta}\right)^{\alpha/(1-\alpha)} AL, \tag{2.23}$$

$$I^* = \delta K^* = \left(\frac{\alpha A}{\rho + \delta}\right)^{1/(1-\alpha)} \delta L, \tag{2.24}$$

$$C^* = Y^* - I^* = \frac{\rho + (1-\alpha)\delta}{\rho + \delta} \left(\frac{\alpha A}{\rho + \delta}\right)^{\alpha/(1-\alpha)} AL. \tag{2.25}$$

2. Consider a positive capital depreciation rate $\delta > 0$. Compute the elasticity of $\{K^*, Y^*, I^*, C^*\}$ with respect to technology A.
3. How does an increase in the capital depreciation rate δ affect the steady-state consumption rate C^*/Y^*? What happens to this effect as $\alpha \to 0$?
4. Suppose the household has the following instantaneous utility function:

$$u_t = \frac{C_t^{1-\sigma} - 1}{1 - \sigma},$$

where $\sigma > 0$ determines the elasticity of intertemporal substitution as $1/\sigma$. This functional form is known as the isoelastic utility function. When $\sigma \to 1$, u_t becomes $\ln C_t$. Show that the optimal consumption path is given by

$$\frac{\dot{C}_t}{C_t} = \frac{1}{\sigma}(R_t - \delta - \rho),$$

in which the change in the growth rate of consumption with respect to a change in the return to capital is determined by $1/\sigma$.

Chapter 3

Dynamics in the Neoclassical Growth Model

In Chapter 2, we focused on the steady state of the neoclassical growth model. In other words, we only looked at the long-run effects of changes in the level of technology. In this chapter, we use a graphical approach to demonstrate the short-run effects of technology, which is a potential source of economic fluctuations in business cycles. We also graphically demonstrate the long-run effects of technology for a comparison with its short-run effects. This analysis enables us to compare the effects of changes in the level of technology on the macroeconomy at different time horizons. In summary, we find that the short-run and long-run supply curves of capital are drastically different, which in turn have interesting implications on the macroeconomic effects of technology.

3.1. Short-Run Effects of Technology

We define the short run as the moment when a parameter (e.g., the level of technology A) changes. At this moment, the level of capital K_t in the economy is predetermined and cannot be changed immediately. In other words, the short-run supply curve of capital is vertical. The assumption of perfectly inelastic supply of labour (i.e., $L_t = L$ for all t) implies that the labour supply curve is also vertical. As for the demand curves of capital and labour, they are given by[1]

$$R_t = \alpha A \left(\frac{L_t}{K_t}\right)^{1-\alpha}, \tag{3.1}$$

$$W_t = (1-\alpha)A \left(\frac{K_t}{L_t}\right)^{\alpha}, \tag{3.2}$$

which equate the rental price R_t to the marginal product of capital and the wage rate W_t to the marginal product of labour.

An increase in the level of technology A shifts the demand curves of capital and labour to the right. As a result, the wage rate W_t and the rental price R_t go up. However, given the vertical supply curves of capital and labour, the levels of capital and labour do not change in the short run; see Figures 3.1 and 3.2.

Then, the production function

$$Y_t = AK_t^{\alpha}L_t^{1-\alpha}, \tag{3.3}$$

implies that an increase in technology A gives rise to an increase in the level of output Y_t despite the fact that capital and labour do not

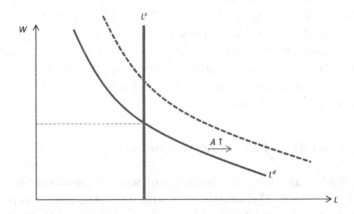

Figure 3.1.   Labour market in the short run.

[1]Recall that we have normalised P_t to unity.

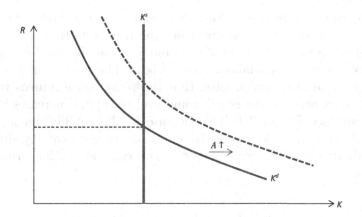

Figure 3.2.   Capital market in the short run.

change in the short run. The short-run effects of technology A can be summarised as follows:

Short-run effects of an increase in A				
Y	K	R	L	W
increase	no change	increase	no change	increase

3.2.   Long-Run Effects of Technology

In the long run, the level of capital fully adjusts to its steady-state equilibrium level. So, what does the long-run supply curve of capital look like? Recall that the optimal consumption path derived from the household's utility maximisation is given by

$$\frac{\dot{C}_t}{C_t} = R_t - \rho, \tag{3.4}$$

where the parameter $\rho > 0$ is the household's discount rate. In the steady state, we have $\dot{C}_t = 0$. Therefore, the steady-state version of the optimal consumption path is given by

$$R_t = \rho, \tag{3.5}$$

which gives us a *horizontal* long-run supply curve of capital. In other words, the long-run supply curve of capital is perfectly elastic.

The increase in the level of technology A has shifted the demand curves of capital and labour to the right. The horizontal long-run supply curve of capital implies that the rental price returns to the initial level whereas the equilibrium level of capital increases in the long run; see Figure 3.4. The increase in the equilibrium level of capital has an additional positive effect on the wage rate by shifting the labour demand curve further to the right in the long run; see Figure 3.3.

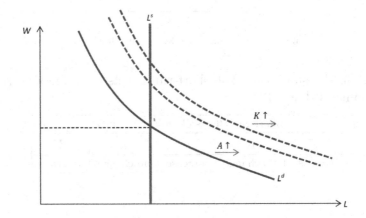

Figure 3.3.   Labour market in the long run.

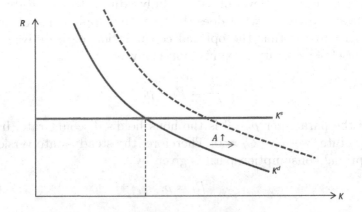

Figure 3.4.   Capital market in the long run.

Then, the production function $Y_t = AK_t^{\alpha}L_t^{1-\alpha}$ implies that the increases in technology A and capital K both give rise to an increase in the steady-state equilibrium level of output Y^*. Furthermore, the increase in the steady-state equilibrium level of capital K^* implies that the long-run increases in the level of output and the wage rate are larger than their short-run increases. The long-run effects of technology A can be summarised as follows:

Long-run effects of an increase in A				
Y	K	R	L	W
increase	increase	no change	no change	increase

3.3. Dynamics

We can also predict what happens as the economy moves from the short run to the long run.[2] After the level of technology A increases, the level of output Y_t increases immediately whereas the level of capital K_t increases gradually, which leads to a further gradual increase in output Y_t; see Figures 3.5 and 3.6. As we move along the capital demand curve, the rental price R_t gradually decreases towards the initial level; see Figure 3.7. The increase in the level of capital gradually shifts the labour demand curve further to the right. As we move along the labour supply curve, the wage rate W_t increases further and gradually converges towards the new steady-state equilibrium level; see Figure 3.8.

3.4. Summary

In this chapter, we use a graphical approach to examine the effects of technology in the neoclassical growth model. We find that the effects of permanent changes in the level of technology vary across time because the short-run and long-run supply curves of capital are very different. In the short run, the capital supply curve is perfectly inelastic, so that changes in the level of technology do not affect the

---

[2]For a more precise analysis, one could use the phase diagram of (2.15) and (2.16) to explore the dynamics of the economy.

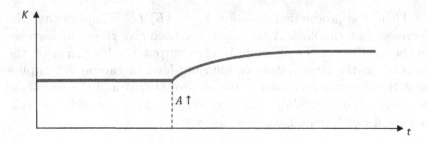

Figure 3.5.   Time path of capital.

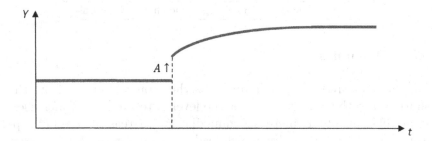

Figure 3.6.   Time path of output.

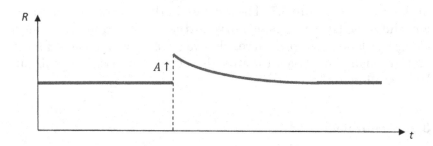

Figure 3.7.   Time path of rental price.

equilibrium level of capital. In this case, an increase in the level of technology increases the level of output, the wage rate and the rental price without affecting the equilibrium levels of labour and capital. In the long run, the capital supply curve becomes perfectly elastic, so that an increase in the level of technology raises the equilibrium level of capital, which in turn has a general-equilibrium effect on the labour market by shifting the labour demand curve further to the right and

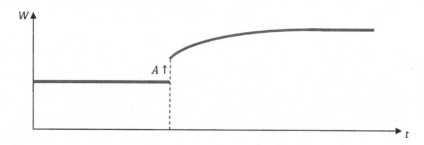

Figure 3.8. Time path of wage rate.

causing a larger increase in the wage rate. In this case, an increase in the level of technology increases the level of output, the wage rate and the equilibrium level of capital without affecting the rental price and the equilibrium level of labour (due to the assumption of perfectly inelastic labour supply). Finally, an unrealistic implication of the neoclassical growth model is that the level of labour (i.e., employment) never changes. In the next chapter, we will consider elastic labour supply.

3.5. Exercises

1. What are the short-run and long-run effects of an increase in the level of labour supply L on $\{Y_t, K_t, R_t, W_t\}$?
2. What are the short-run and long-run effects of an increase in the household's discount rate ρ on $\{Y_t, K_t, R_t, W_t\}$?
3. Consider a positive capital depreciation rate $\delta > 0$. Derive the long-run capital supply curve. How does the capital depreciation rate δ affect the long-run capital supply curve?

Chapter 4

The Neoclassical Growth Model with Elastic Labour Supply

In Chapter 3, we considered perfectly inelastic labour supply in the neoclassical growth model, in which case the level of labour (i.e., employment) never changes. In this chapter, we generalise the neoclassical growth model to allow for elastic labour supply chosen by the utility-maximising household.[1] In summary, the supply of labour is determined by a substitution effect and an income effect, which are both influenced by changes in technology. Therefore, this modification of elastic labour supply allows for fluctuations in employment, which are an important feature of business cycles. The neoclassical growth model with elastic labour supply is essentially a special case of the real business cycle (RBC) model.[2]

4.1. Household

We introduce the choice of leisure into the household's utility function:

$$U = \int_0^\infty e^{-\rho t}[\ln C_t + \beta \ln(L - l_t)]dt, \qquad (4.1)$$

---

[1]See Romer (2018, chapter 11) for other approaches of modelling unemployment.

[2]The RBC model was developed by Kydland and Prescott (1982), who received the Nobel Memorial Prize in Economics in 2004 partly for this contribution. See McCandless (2008) and Romer (2018, chapter 5) for a textbook treatment of the RBC model.

where the parameter $\rho > 0$ is the household's discount rate and the parameter $\beta > 0$ determines the importance of leisure $L - l_t$ relative to consumption C_t in the utility function. L is the household's total labour endowment, and l_t is the level of employment chosen by the household. The household elastically supplies l_t units of labour to earn a wage income W_t. Furthermore, it accumulates capital K_t and rents it to the representative firm to earn a capital-rental income R_t. The asset-accumulation equation is modified as follows:

$$\dot{K}_t = R_t K_t + W_t l_t - C_t, \tag{4.2}$$

where we have assumed a zero depreciation rate of capital (i.e., $\delta = 0$).[3]

4.2.   Hamiltonian

The Hamiltonian function is given by

$$H_t = \ln C_t + \beta \ln(L - l_t) + \lambda_t(R_t K_t + W_t l_t - C_t). \tag{4.3}$$

The first-order conditions include

$$\frac{\partial H_t}{\partial l_t} = -\frac{\beta}{L - l_t} + \lambda_t W_t = 0, \tag{4.4}$$

$$\frac{\partial H_t}{\partial C_t} = \frac{1}{C_t} - \lambda_t = 0, \tag{4.5}$$

$$\frac{\partial H_t}{\partial K_t} = \lambda_t R_t = \lambda_t \rho - \dot{\lambda}_t. \tag{4.6}$$

Recall that K_t is a state variable (i.e., a variable that accumulates over time), so we have to set $\partial H_t / \partial K_t = \lambda_t \rho - \dot{\lambda}_t$.

Combining (4.4) and (4.5) yields the labour supply curve l_t^s given by

$$l_t^s = L - \frac{\beta C_t}{W_t}, \tag{4.7}$$

which is increasing in the wage rate W_t (i.e., a substitution effect) and decreasing in consumption C_t (i.e., an income effect). Intuitively, a

---

[3]In general, the asset-accumulation equation is given by $\dot{K}_t = (R_t - \delta)K_t + W_t l_t - C_t$.

higher wage rate increases the opportunity cost of leisure and causes the household to supply more labour, which captures a substitution effect, whereas a higher level of consumption decreases the marginal utility of consumption from wage income and causes the household to enjoy more leisure, which captures an income effect. If leisure is not important to the household (i.e., $\beta = 0$), then we have $l_t^s = L$, in which case we are back to the case of perfectly inelastic labour supply in the previous chapter. If leisure matters to the household (i.e., $\beta > 0$), then unemployment $L - l_t^s$ is positive. Taking the log of (4.5) and substituting it into (4.6) yields the optimal consumption path:

$$\frac{\dot{C}_t}{C_t} = R_t - \rho, \tag{4.8}$$

which is the same as in the previous chapter.

4.3. Firm

The firm's optimisation problem is the same as before. There is a representative firm in the economy, and this firm hires labour and rents capital from the household to produce output using the following production function:

$$Y_t = AK_t^\alpha l_t^{1-\alpha}, \tag{4.9}$$

where the parameter $\alpha \in (0,1)$ is the degree of capital intensity in production and A is the exogenous level of technology. The profit function Π_t is

$$\Pi_t = Y_t - R_t K_t - W_t l_t, \tag{4.10}$$

where we have chosen Y_t as the numeraire (i.e., the price of Y_t is normalised to unity). Differentiating (4.10) with respect to K_t and l_t yields

$$\frac{\partial \Pi_t}{\partial K_t} = \frac{\partial Y_t}{\partial K_t} - R_t = \alpha A \left(\frac{l_t}{K_t} \right)^{1-\alpha} - R_t = 0, \tag{4.11}$$

$$\frac{\partial \Pi_t}{\partial l_t} = \frac{\partial Y_t}{\partial l_t} - W_t = (1 - \alpha) A \left(\frac{K_t}{l_t} \right)^{\alpha} - W_t = 0. \tag{4.12}$$

These two equations are the demand functions for K_t and l_t.

4.4. Short-Run Effects of Technology

Once again, we define the short run as the moment when a parameter (e.g., the level of technology A) changes. At this moment, the level of capital in the economy is predetermined. In other words, the short-run supply curve of capital is vertical as before. However, we now have an upward-sloping labour supply curve given by

$$W_t = \frac{\beta C_t}{L - l_t}. \tag{4.13}$$

As for the demand curves of labour and capital, they are given by

$$R_t = \alpha A \left(\frac{l_t}{K_t}\right)^{1-\alpha} = \alpha \frac{Y_t}{K_t}, \tag{4.14}$$

$$W_t = (1 - \alpha)A \left(\frac{K_t}{l_t}\right)^{\alpha} = (1 - \alpha)\frac{Y_t}{l_t}. \tag{4.15}$$

An increase in the level of technology A shifts the demand curves of labour and capital to the right. In the labour market, the wage rate W_t and the equilibrium level of labour l_t increase.[4] Therefore, elastic labour supply gives rise to a positive effect of technology A on employment l_t, which in turn has a general-equilibrium effect on the capital market. In the capital market, the rental price R_t increases, whereas the equilibrium level of capital does not change in the short run; see Figures 4.1 and 4.2.

Then, the production function

$$Y_t = AK_t^{\alpha}l_t^{1-\alpha} \tag{4.16}$$

implies that the increases in technology A and labour l_t both give rise to an increase in the level of output Y_t. The short-run effects of technology A can be summarised as follows:

Short-run effects of an increase in A				
Y	K	R	l	W
increase	no change	increase	increase	increase

---

[4]Technically, the labour supply curve may shift due to changes in consumption C_t. We ignore this effect in the short run.

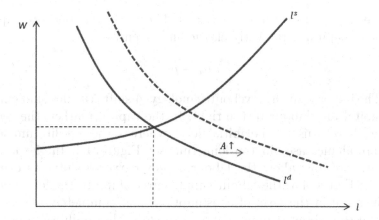

Figure 4.1. Labour market in the short run.

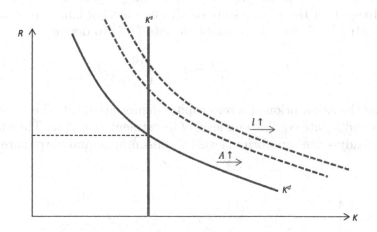

Figure 4.2. Capital market in the short run.

4.5. Long-Run Effects of Technology

In the long run, the level of capital fully adjusts to its steady-state equilibrium level K^*. Recall that the optimal consumption path is given by

$$\frac{\dot{C_t}}{C_t} = R_t - \rho. \tag{4.17}$$

In the steady state, we have $\dot{C}_t = 0$. Therefore, the long-run supply curve of capital is perfectly elastic and given by

$$R_t = \rho. \tag{4.18}$$

The increase in the level of technology A shifts the demand curves of capital and labour to the right. In the capital market, the rental price R_t returns to the initial level whereas the equilibrium level of capital increases in the long run; see Figure 4.4. In the labour market, we now allow the labour supply curve to shift. As can be seen in Figure 4.3, the labour supply curve shifts to the left (due to an increase in the level of consumption) and completely offsets the shift in the labour demand curve. Therefore, the equilibrium level of labour l_t returns to the initial level. However, there continues to be a positive effect on the wage rate W_t in the long run; see Figure 4.3.

To see that the steady-state equilibrium level of labour returns to the initial level, we substitute (4.15) into (4.7) to derive

$$l_t = L - \frac{\beta C_t}{W_t} = L - \frac{\beta C_t}{(1-\alpha)Y_t}l_t. \tag{4.19}$$

Given the assumption of a zero capital depreciation rate (i.e., $\delta = 0$), the steady-state equilibrium level of investment I^* is zero. Therefore, the steady-state equilibrium levels of consumption and output are the

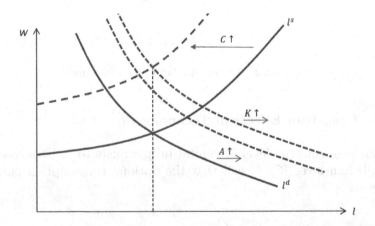

Figure 4.3.   Labour market in the long run.

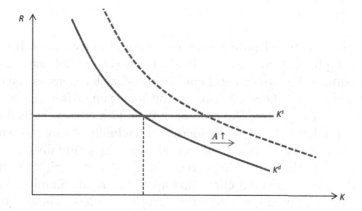

Figure 4.4. Capital market in the long run.

same such that $C^* = Y^*$. Therefore, (4.19) implies that the steady-state equilibrium level of labour l^* is given by

$$l^* = \frac{L}{1 + \beta/(1 - \alpha)}, \qquad (4.20)$$

which is independent of technology A. In other words, changes in the level of technology A do not affect the steady-state equilibrium level of labour l^*. Furthermore, the steady-state equilibrium level of labour l^* is decreasing in leisure preference β and capital intensity α. Intuitively, if leisure becomes more important (i.e., a larger β) to the household, it would supply less labour to the labour market. Similarly, if labour becomes less important in production (i.e., a larger α), the firm would demand less labour in the labour market.

Finally, the production function $Y_t = AK_t^\alpha l_t^{1-\alpha}$ implies that the increases in technology A and capital K both give rise to an increase in the steady-state equilibrium level of output Y^*. Furthermore, the increase in the steady-state equilibrium level of capital K^* and the leftward shift in the labour supply curve imply that the long-run increase in the wage rate is larger than its short-run increase. The long-run effects of technology A can be summarised as follows:

Long-run effects of an increase in A				
Y	K	R	l	W
increase	increase	no change	no change	increase

4.6. Dynamics

Given the additional adjustment in labour, the dynamics becomes more complicated in the neoclassical growth model with elastic labour supply, but we can still conjecture what happens as the economy moves from the short run to the long run. After the level of technology A increases, the level of output Y_t increases immediately whereas the level of capital K_t increases gradually. As we move along the capital demand curve, the rental price R_t gradually decreases towards the initial level. The increase in the level of capital gradually shifts the labour demand curve further to the right. Simultaneously, the labour supply curve gradually shifts to the left. These shifts in the labour demand and supply curves give rise to a gradual increase in the wage rate W_t towards the new steady-state equilibrium level and a gradual decrease in the level of labour l_t towards the initial level.

4.7. Summary

In this chapter, we extend the neoclassical growth model by allowing for elastic labour supply. In the model, the representative household chooses leisure in addition to consumption and saving. Maximising the household's utility, we derive the labour supply curve. The household's supply of labour is increasing in the wage rate, which captures a substitution effect, and decreasing in the level of consumption, which captures an income effect. Given the upward-sloping labour supply curve, an increase in the level of technology shifts the labour demand curve to the right and increases the equilibrium level of labour in the short run, which in turn has a general-equilibrium effect on the capital market by shifting the capital demand curve further to the right and causing a larger increase in the rental price. In this case, an increase in the level of technology increases the level of output, the level of labour, the wage rate and the rental price without affecting the level of capital in the short run. In the long run, the higher level of consumption gives rise to an income effect on labour supply and shifts the labour supply curve to the left. As a result, the equilibrium level of labour returns to the initial level. However, the long-run capital supply curve becomes perfectly elastic, and the equilibrium level of capital increases in the long run. In this case, an increase in the level of technology increases the level of output, the level of capital and the wage rate without affecting the rental price and the level of labour in the long run.

4.8. Exercises

1. Consider a positive capital depreciation rate $\delta > 0$. In this case, the asset-accumulation equation becomes

$$\dot{K}_t = (R_t - \delta)K_t + W_t l_t - C_t. \qquad (4.21)$$

Show that the steady-state equilibrium level of labour l^* is given by[5]

$$l^* = \frac{L}{1 + \frac{\beta}{1-\alpha}\left(1 - \frac{\alpha\delta}{\rho+\delta}\right)}, \qquad (4.22)$$

which continues to be independent of technology A. In other words, changes in the level of technology A do not affect the steady-state equilibrium level of labour l^* even in the presence of capital depreciation. Furthermore, (4.22) shows that the steady-state equilibrium level of labour l^* is increasing in the capital depreciation rate δ and decreasing in the discount rate ρ. Intuitively, an increase in the capital depreciation rate δ or a decrease in the discount rate ρ reduces the consumption rate C/Y, which in turn decreases leisure and increases labour.

2. Derive the steady-state equilibrium levels of capital K^* and output Y^*.

3. Consider an alternative utility function given by

$$U = \int_0^\infty e^{-\rho t} \left(\ln C_t - \beta l_t\right) dt. \qquad (4.23)$$

Show that the labour supply curve becomes perfectly elastic. How does an increase in consumption C_t shift the labour supply curve?

---

[5]Hint: Note that $C^*/Y^* = 1 - I^*/Y^* = 1 - \delta K^*/Y^*$.

4. Consider the following household's lifetime utility function:

$$U = \int_0^\infty e^{-\rho t} \left(\ln C_t - \frac{l_t^{1+\varphi}}{1+\varphi} \right) dt,$$

where $\varphi > 0$. Derive the labour supply curve.

Chapter 5

Fiscal Policy: Government Spending

The neoclassical growth model not only allows us to analyse the effects of technology but also allows us to perform policy analysis. We now begin our analysis of government policies in the neoclassical growth model. We will consider a number of fiscal policy instruments in this chapter and the following chapters. The policy instrument that we consider in this chapter is government spending.[1] Specifically, we analyse the macroeconomic effects of changes in government spending in the neoclassical growth model with elastic labour supply, which is a crucial feature because the expansionary effects of government spending operate through an income effect on labour supply.

5.1. Household

The representative household's utility function U is given by[2]

$$U = \int_0^\infty e^{-\rho t} [\ln C_t + \beta \ln(L - l_t)] dt, \qquad (5.1)$$

---

[1] Here we only consider permanent changes in government spending; see Baxter and King (1993) for a comparison between permanent versus temporary changes in government spending in the neoclassical growth model.

[2] We can generalise the utility function to allow government spending G_t to improve the household's utility; e.g., $U = \int_0^\infty e^{-\rho t} [\ln C_t + \theta \ln(L - l_t) + V(G_t)] dt$. All our results would hold so long as G_t does not affect the marginal utility of consumption and leisure.

where the parameter $\rho > 0$ is the household's discount rate and the parameter $\beta > 0$ determines the importance of leisure $L - l_t$ relative to consumption C_t in the utility function. L is the household's total labour endowment, and l_t is the level of employment chosen by the household. The household elastically supplies l_t units of labour to earn a wage income W_t. Furthermore, it accumulates capital K_t and rents it to the representative firm to earn a capital-rental income R_t. The asset-accumulation equation is

$$\dot{K}_t = R_t K_t + W_t l_t - C_t - T_t, \qquad (5.2)$$

where the capital depreciation rate is zero and T_t is a lump-sum tax.[3]

5.2.   Government

The government collects tax revenue T_t to pay for government spending G_t. The balanced budget condition is $G_t = T_t$. We define the ratio of government spending to output as $\gamma \equiv G_t/Y_t$. We are interested in the effects of changes in γ on other macroeconomic variables.

5.3.   Hamiltonian

The Hamiltonian function of the household is given by

$$H_t = \ln C_t + \beta \ln(L - l_t) + \lambda_t(R_t K_t + W_t l_t - C_t - T_t). \qquad (5.3)$$

The first-order conditions include

$$\frac{\partial H_t}{\partial l_t} = -\frac{\beta}{L - l_t} + \lambda_t W_t = 0, \qquad (5.4)$$

$$\frac{\partial H_t}{\partial C_t} = \frac{1}{C_t} - \lambda_t = 0, \qquad (5.5)$$

$$\frac{\partial H_t}{\partial K_t} = \lambda_t R_t = \lambda_t \rho - \dot{\lambda}_t. \qquad (5.6)$$

Recall that K_t is a state variable (i.e., a variable that accumulates over time), so we have to set $\partial H_t/\partial K_t = \lambda_t \rho - \dot{\lambda}_t$.

---

[3]We will consider other tax instruments in the next two chapters.

Combining (5.4) and (5.5) yields the labour supply curve l_t^s given by

$$l_t^s = L - \frac{\beta C_t}{W_t}, \tag{5.7}$$

which is increasing in the wage rate W_t (i.e., a substitution effect) and decreasing in consumption C_t (i.e., an income effect). Unless $\beta = 0$, unemployment $L - l_t^s$ is positive. Taking the log of (5.5) and substituting it into (5.6) yields the optimal consumption path:

$$\frac{\dot{C}_t}{C_t} = R_t - \rho. \tag{5.8}$$

In summary, the labour supply curve and the optimal consumption path are the same as before.

5.4. Firm

The firm's optimisation problem is also the same as before. There is a representative firm in the economy, and this firm hires labour l_t and rents capital K_t from the household to produce output Y_t using the following Cobb–Douglas production function:

$$Y_t = AK_t^\alpha l_t^{1-\alpha}, \tag{5.9}$$

where the parameter $\alpha \in (0,1)$ is the degree of capital intensity in production and A is the exogenous level of technology. The profit function Π_t is

$$\Pi_t = Y_t - R_t K_t - W_t l_t, \tag{5.10}$$

where we have implicitly chosen Y_t as the numeraire (i.e., the price of Y_t is normalised to unity). Differentiating (5.10) with respect to K_t and l_t yields

$$\frac{\partial \Pi_t}{\partial K_t} = \frac{\partial Y_t}{\partial K_t} - R_t = \alpha A \left(\frac{l_t}{K_t} \right)^{1-\alpha} - R_t = 0, \tag{5.11}$$

$$\frac{\partial \Pi_t}{\partial l_t} = \frac{\partial Y_t}{\partial l_t} - W_t = (1-\alpha)A \left(\frac{K_t}{l_t} \right)^\alpha - W_t = 0. \tag{5.12}$$

These two equations are the demand functions for K_t and l_t. In summary, the demand functions for K_t and l_t are also the same as before.

5.5.   Long-Run Effects of Government Spending

We start with the long-run effects of permanent changes in government spending. In the long run, the level of capital fully adjusts to its steady-state equilibrium level. Recall that the optimal consumption path is given by

$$\frac{\dot{C}_t}{C_t} = R_t - \rho. \tag{5.13}$$

In the steady state, we have $\dot{C}_t = 0$. Therefore, the long-run supply curve of capital is perfectly elastic and given by

$$R_t = \rho, \tag{5.14}$$

whereas the labour supply curve is

$$W_t = \frac{\beta C_t}{L - l_t}. \tag{5.15}$$

As for the demand curves of capital and labour, they are given by

$$R_t = \alpha A \left(\frac{l_t}{K_t}\right)^{1-\alpha} = \alpha \frac{Y_t}{K_t}, \tag{5.16}$$

$$W_t = (1 - \alpha)A \left(\frac{K_t}{l_t}\right)^{\alpha} = (1 - \alpha)\frac{Y_t}{l_t}. \tag{5.17}$$

Combining labour supply in (5.15) and labour demand in (5.17) yields

$$l_t = L - \frac{\beta C_t}{W_t} = L - \frac{\beta C_t}{(1 - \alpha)Y_t}l_t. \tag{5.18}$$

Given the assumption of a zero capital depreciation rate (i.e., $\delta = 0$), the steady-state equilibrium level of investment I^* is zero. Therefore, the steady-state equilibrium level of consumption is given by

$$C^* = Y^* - G^* = (1 - \gamma)Y^*, \tag{5.19}$$

which is proportional to the steady-state equilibrium level of output. Substituting (5.19) into (5.18) yields the steady-state equilibrium level of labour l^* given by

$$l^* = \frac{L}{1 + \beta(1 - \gamma)/(1 - \alpha)}, \tag{5.20}$$

which is increasing in the government-spending ratio γ.

Intuitively, an increase in government spending γ raises tax T and reduces the after-tax income to cause a negative income effect on the household, which then consumes less leisure and supplies more labour l. Graphically, it shifts the labour supply curve to the right; as a result, the equilibrium level of labour l increases and the wage rate W decreases; see Figure 5.1. In the capital market, the increase in the level of labour shifts the capital demand curve to the right. Given the horizontal long-run capital supply curve, the rental price R remains at the initial level whereas the equilibrium level of capital increases in the long run; see Figure 5.2. The increase in capital shifts the labour demand curve to the right. As a result, the wage rate W

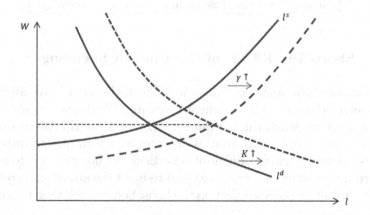

Figure 5.1. Labour market in the long run.

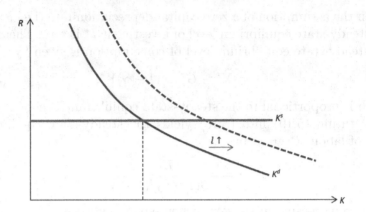

Figure 5.2.   Capital market in the long run.

increases and returns to the initial level because the capital–labour ratio K/l is independent of γ.[4]

Finally, the production function $Y_t = AK_t^\alpha l_t^{1-\alpha}$ implies that the increases in labour and capital both give rise to an increase in the steady-state equilibrium level of output Y^*. The long-run effects of government spending γ can be summarised as follows:

Long-run effects of an increase in γ				
Y	K	R	l	W
increase	increase	no change	increase	no change

5.6.   Short-Run Effects of Government Spending

To complete our analysis, we now look at the short-run effects of permanent changes in government spending. We define the short run as the moment when the parameter γ changes. At this moment, the level of capital in the economy is predetermined. In other words, the short-run supply curve of capital is vertical. As before, an increase in government spending γ raises tax and reduces the after-tax income to cause a negative income effect on the household, which then consumes

---

[4]Note from (5.17) that W is increasing in K/l. Then, note from (5.16) that R is decreasing in K/l and $R = \rho$ does not change in the steady state.

less leisure and supplies more labour. Graphically, it shifts the labour supply curve to the right; as a result, the equilibrium level of labour increases and the wage rate decreases; see Figure 5.3. In the capital market, the increase in the level of labour shifts the capital demand curve to the right. Given the vertical short-run capital supply curve, the rental price increases whereas the equilibrium level of capital remains unchanged in the short run; see Figure 5.4. Finally, the production function $Y_t = AK_t^\alpha l_t^{1-\alpha}$ implies that the increase in labour

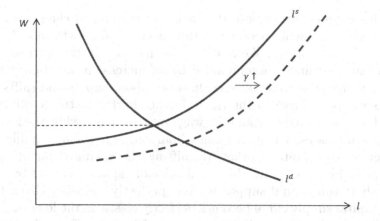

Figure 5.3.   Labour market in the short run.

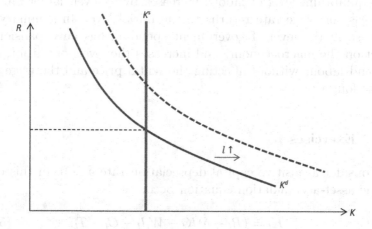

Figure 5.4.   Capital market in the short run.

gives rise to an increase in the level of output. The short-run effects of government spending γ can be summarised as follows:

Short-run effects of an increase in γ				
Y	K	R	l	W
increase	no change	increase	increase	decrease

5.7.   Summary

In this chapter, we explore the effects of permanent changes in the level of government spending in the neoclassical growth model with elastic labour supply. We find that an increase in the level of government spending is accompanied by an increase in taxation, which in turn gives rise to an income effect on labour supply and shifts the labour supply curve to the right. In the short run, the equilibrium level of labour increases and the wage rate decreases while the level of output increases. The increase in labour causes a general-equilibrium effect on the capital market by shifting the capital demand curve to the right. As a result, the rental price of capital increases because the short-run capital supply curve is perfectly inelastic. Given that the capital supply curve becomes perfectly elastic in the long run, the equilibrium level of capital increases and in turn affects the labour market by shifting the labour demand curve to the right. At the end, the equilibrium level of labour increases by an even larger amount whereas the wage rate returns to the initial level. In summary, an increase in the level of government spending has an expansionary effect on the macroeconomy and increases the levels of output, capital and labour without affecting the rental price and the wage rate in the long run.

5.8.   Exercises

1. Consider a positive capital depreciation rate $\delta > 0$. In this case, the asset-accumulation equation becomes

$$\dot{K}_t = (R_t - \delta)K_t + W_t l_t - C_t - T_t. \qquad (5.21)$$

Show that the steady-state equilibrium level of labour l^* is given by

$$l^* = \frac{L}{1 + \frac{\beta}{1-\alpha}\left(1 - \gamma - \frac{\alpha\delta}{\rho+\delta}\right)}, \tag{5.22}$$

which continues to be increasing in the government-spending ratio γ.

2. Derive the steady-state equilibrium levels of capital K^* and output Y^*.
3. What are the long-run effects of government spending γ on consumption and investment?
4. Consider the following government's budget constraint:

$$T_t = G_t + TR_t = \gamma Y_t + TR_t,$$

where TR_t is the transfer payment from the government to the household. In this case, the household's asset-accumulation equation is given by

$$\dot{K}_t = R_t K_t + W_t l_t - C_t - T_t + TR_t.$$

Suppose the lump-sum tax T_t is fixed, and the transfer payment of government TR_t adjusts endogenously to offset the change in γ and balance the government's budget constraint. Does the presence of TR_t cause any difference to the effects of γ on the labour and capital markets in the short run and long run?

Chapter 6

Fiscal Policy: Labour Income Tax

In this chapter, we continue our analysis of fiscal policies in the neoclassical growth model. In Chapter 5, we considered a lump-sum tax, which is a very rare fiscal policy instrument in reality. Therefore, we now consider a labour income tax, which is a more realistic tax instrument. Once again, we use in this policy analysis the neoclassical growth model with elastic labour supply, which is a crucial feature because the contractionary effects of labour income tax operate through a substitution effect on labour supply.

6.1. Household

As before, the household's utility function is given by

$$U = \int_0^\infty e^{-\rho t}[\ln C_t + \beta \ln(L - l_t)]dt, \tag{6.1}$$

where the parameter $\rho > 0$ is the household's discount rate and the parameter $\beta > 0$ determines the importance of leisure $L - l_t$ relative to consumption C_t in the utility function. L is the household's total labour endowment, and l_t is the level of employment chosen by the household. The household elastically supplies l_t units of labour to earn an after-tax wage income $(1 - \tau_W)W_t$, where $\tau_W > 0$ is the tax rate on labour income. Furthermore, the household accumulates capital K_t and rents it to the representative firm to earn a capital-rental income R_t. The asset-accumulation equation is

$$\dot{K}_t = R_t K_t + (1 - \tau_W) W_t l_t - C_t - T_t, \tag{6.2}$$

where the capital depreciation rate is zero and T_t is a lump-sum tax.

6.2. Government

The government collects tax revenue to pay for government spending G_t. The balanced budget condition is $G_t = T_t + \tau_W W_t l_t$. We define the ratio of government spending to output as $\gamma \equiv G_t/Y_t$. We are interested in the effects of changes in the labour income tax rate τ_W on other macroeconomic variables. In the previous chapter, we saw that changes in G_t cause an income effect on the household. To separate this income effect from our analysis, we assume that changes in the labour income tax rate τ_W are balanced by changes in the lump-sum tax T_t while the government-spending ratio γ does not change. Therefore, changes in the labour income tax rate τ_W only give rise to a substitution effect on the household's labour supply.

6.3. Hamiltonian

The Hamiltonian function of the household is given by

$$H_t = \ln C_t + \beta \ln(L - l_t) + \lambda_t [R_t K_t + (1 - \tau_W) W_t l_t - C_t - T_t]. \tag{6.3}$$

The first-order conditions include

$$\frac{\partial H_t}{\partial l_t} = -\frac{\beta}{L - l_t} + \lambda_t (1 - \tau_W) W_t = 0, \tag{6.4}$$

$$\frac{\partial H_t}{\partial C_t} = \frac{1}{C_t} - \lambda_t = 0, \tag{6.5}$$

$$\frac{\partial H_t}{\partial K_t} = \lambda_t R_t = \lambda_t \rho - \dot{\lambda}_t. \tag{6.6}$$

Recall that K_t is a state variable (i.e., a variable that accumulates over time), so we have to set $\partial H_t/\partial K_t = \lambda_t \rho - \dot{\lambda}_t$. Combining (6.4) and (6.5) yields the labour supply curve l_t^s given by

$$l_t^s = L - \frac{\beta C_t}{(1 - \tau_W)W_t},\tag{6.7}$$

which is increasing in the wage rate W_t but decreasing in the labour income tax rate τ_W. Taking the log of (6.5) and substituting it into (6.6) yields the optimal consumption path:

$$\frac{\dot{C}_t}{C_t} = R_t - \rho.\tag{6.8}$$

In summary, the optimal consumption path is the same as before, whereas the labour supply curve now depends on the after-tax wage rate $(1 - \tau_W)W_t$.

6.4. Firm

The firm's optimisation problem is the same as before. There is a representative firm in the economy, and this firm hires labour and rents capital from the household to produce output using the following production function:

$$Y_t = AK_t^\alpha l_t^{1-\alpha},\tag{6.9}$$

where the parameter $\alpha \in (0,1)$ is the degree of capital intensity in production and A is the exogenous level of technology. The profit function Π_t is

$$\Pi_t = Y_t - R_t K_t - W_t l_t,\tag{6.10}$$

where we have implicitly chosen Y_t as the numeraire (i.e., the price of Y_t is normalised to unity). Differentiating (6.10) with respect to K_t and l_t yields

$$\frac{\partial \Pi_t}{\partial K_t} = \frac{\partial Y_t}{\partial K_t} - R_t = \alpha A \left(\frac{l_t}{K_t}\right)^{1-\alpha} - R_t = 0,\tag{6.11}$$

$$\frac{\partial \Pi_t}{\partial l_t} = \frac{\partial Y_t}{\partial l_t} - W_t = (1-\alpha)A \left(\frac{K_t}{l_t}\right)^\alpha - W_t = 0.\tag{6.12}$$

These two equations are the demand functions for K_t and l_t. In summary, the demand functions for K_t and l_t are also the same as before.

6.5. Long-Run Effects of Labour Income Tax

We start with the long-run effects of labour income tax. In the long run, the level of capital fully adjusts to its steady-state equilibrium level. Recall that the optimal consumption path is given by

$$\frac{\dot{C}_t}{C_t} = R_t - \rho. \tag{6.13}$$

In the steady state, we have $\dot{C}_t = 0$. Therefore, the long-run supply curve of capital is perfectly elastic and given by

$$R_t = \rho, \tag{6.14}$$

whereas the labour supply curve is

$$W_t = \frac{1}{1 - \tau_W} \frac{\beta C_t}{L - l_t}. \tag{6.15}$$

As for the demand curves of capital and labour, they are given by

$$R_t = \alpha A \left(\frac{l_t}{K_t} \right)^{1-\alpha} = \alpha \frac{Y_t}{K_t}, \tag{6.16}$$

$$W_t = (1 - \alpha) A \left(\frac{K_t}{l_t} \right)^{\alpha} = (1 - \alpha) \frac{Y_t}{l_t}. \tag{6.17}$$

Combining labour supply in (6.15) and labour demand in (6.17) yields

$$l_t = L - \frac{\beta C_t}{(1 - \tau_W) W_t} = L - \frac{\beta C_t}{(1 - \tau_W)(1 - \alpha) Y_t} l_t. \tag{6.18}$$

Given the assumption of a zero capital depreciation rate (i.e., $\delta = 0$), the steady-state equilibrium level of investment I^* is zero. Therefore, the steady-state equilibrium level of consumption is given by

$$C^* = Y^* - G^* = (1 - \gamma)Y^*, \tag{6.19}$$

which is proportional to the steady-state equilibrium level of output. Substituting (6.19) into (6.18) yields the steady-state equilibrium level of labour l^* given by

$$l^* = \frac{L}{1 + \frac{\beta}{1-\alpha}\left(\frac{1-\gamma}{1-\tau_W}\right)}, \tag{6.20}$$

which is decreasing in the labour income tax rate τ_W.

Intuitively, an increase in the labour income tax rate τ_W reduces the after-tax wage rate, which in turn causes the household to substitute leisure for consumption (i.e., a substitution effect) and supply less labour l. Graphically, it shifts the labour supply curve to the left; as a result, the equilibrium level of labour l decreases and the pre-tax wage rate W increases; see Figure 6.1. In the capital market, the decrease in the level of labour shifts the capital demand curve to the left. Given the horizontal long-run capital supply curve, the rental price R_t remains at the initial level whereas the equilibrium level of capital decreases in the long run; see Figure 6.2. The decrease in capital shifts the labour demand curve to the left; see Figure 6.1. As a result, the pre-tax wage rate W decreases and returns to the initial

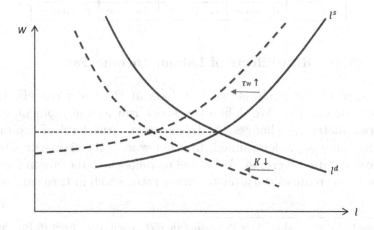

Figure 6.1. Labour market in the long run.

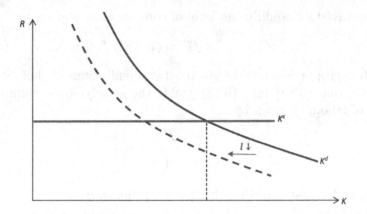

Figure 6.2.   Capital market in the long run.

level because the capital–labour ratio K/l is independent of τ_W.[1]
Although the pre-tax wage rate W does not change in the long run,
the after-tax wage rate $(1 - \tau_W)W$ decreases.

Finally, the production function $Y_t = AK_t^\alpha l_t^{1-\alpha}$ implies that the
decreases in labour and capital both give rise to a decrease in the
steady-state equilibrium level of output Y^*. The long-run effects of
labour income tax τ_W can be summarised as follows:

Long-run effects of an increase in τ_W				
Y	K	R	l	W
decrease	decrease	no change	decrease	no change

6.6.   Short-Run Effects of Labour Income Tax

To complete our analysis, we now look at the short-run effects of
labour income tax. We define the short run as the moment when
the parameter τ_W changes. At this moment, the level of capital in
the economy is predetermined. In other words, the short-run supply
curve of capital is vertical. As before, an increase in the labour income
tax rate τ_W reduces the after-tax wage rate, which in turn causes the

---

[1]Note from (6.17) that W is increasing in K/l. Then, note from (6.16) that R
is decreasing in K/l and $R = \rho$ does not change in the steady state.

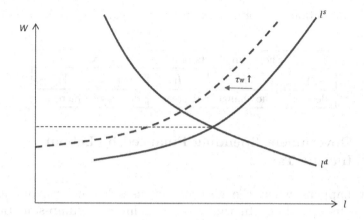

Figure 6.3. Labour market in the short run.

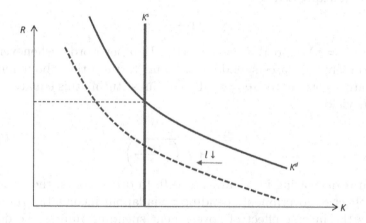

Figure 6.4. Capital market in the short run.

household to substitute leisure for consumption (i.e., a substitution effect) and supply less labour. Graphically, it shifts the labour supply curve to the left; as a result, the equilibrium level of labour decreases and the pre-tax wage rate W increases; see Figure 6.3. In the capital market, the decrease in the level of labour shifts the capital demand curve to the left. Given the vertical short-run capital supply curve, the rental price decreases whereas the equilibrium level of capital remains unchanged in the short run; see Figure 6.4. Finally, the production function $Y_t = AK_t^\alpha l_t^{1-\alpha}$ implies that the decrease in labour gives rise to a decrease in the level of output. The short-run effects of labour income tax rate τ_W can be summarised as follows:

Short-run effects of an increase in τ_W				
Y	K	R	l	W
decrease	no change	decrease	decrease	increase

6.7. Government Spending Financed by Labour Income Tax

What happens when the government uses labour income tax to finance its spending? In this case, we eliminate lump-sum tax T_t and modify the balanced budget condition as $G_t = \tau_W W_t l_t$, which can be re-expressed as

$$\gamma = (1 - \alpha)\tau_W \tag{6.21}$$

using $G_t = \gamma Y_t$ and $W_t l_t = (1 - \alpha)Y_t$. In other words, whenever the government increases spending γ, it has to raise the labour income tax rate according to $\tau_W = \gamma/(1-\alpha)$. Substituting this equation into (6.20) yields

$$l^* = \frac{L}{1 + \beta\left(\frac{1-\gamma}{1-\alpha-\gamma}\right)}, \tag{6.22}$$

which is decreasing in γ unless $\alpha \to 0$. In other words, the substitution effect of government spending γ via labour income tax τ_W dominates the income effect of government spending (unless the degree of capital intensity α approaches zero, in which case they cancel each other). As a result, the steady-state equilibrium levels of capital and output are decreasing in γ.[2]

6.8. Summary

In this chapter, we explore the effects of permanent changes in the labour income tax rate in the neoclassical growth model with elastic

---

[2]Barro and Redlick (2011) provide empirical evidence that the estimated tax multiplier is larger than the spending multiplier in absolute terms such that the overall balanced-budget multiplier for government spending is negative.

labour supply. We find that by decreasing the after-tax wage rate, an increase in labour income tax gives rise to a substitution effect on labour supply and shifts the labour supply curve to the left. In the short run, the equilibrium level of labour decreases and the pre-tax wage rate increases while the level of output decreases. The decrease in labour causes a general-equilibrium effect on the capital market by shifting the capital demand curve to the left. As a result, the rental price of capital decreases because the short-run capital supply curve is perfectly inelastic. Given that the capital supply curve becomes perfectly elastic in the long run, the equilibrium level of capital decreases and in turn affects the labour market by shifting the labour demand curve to the left. At the end, the equilibrium level of labour decreases by an even larger amount whereas the pre-tax wage rate returns to the initial level. In summary, an increase in the labour income tax rate has a contractionary effect on the macroeconomy and decreases the levels of output, capital and labour without affecting the rental price and the pre-tax wage rate in the long run.

6.9. Exercises

1. Consider a positive capital depreciation rate $\delta > 0$. In this case, the asset-accumulation equation becomes

$$\dot{K}_t = (R_t - \delta)K_t + (1 - \tau_W)W_t l_t - C_t - T_t. \tag{6.23}$$

Show that the steady-state equilibrium level of labour l^* is given by

$$l^* = \frac{L}{1 + \frac{\beta}{(1-\alpha)(1-\tau_W)}\left(1 - \gamma - \frac{\alpha\delta}{\rho+\delta}\right)}, \tag{6.24}$$

which is decreasing in the labour income tax rate τ_W for a given γ.[3]

2. Derive the steady-state equilibrium levels of capital K^* and output Y^*.

---

[3]Substituting $\tau_W = \gamma/(1 - \alpha)$ into (6.24), one can show that l^* continues to be decreasing in γ as in Section 6.7 unless $\alpha \to 0$ or $\rho \to 0$.

3. What are the long-run effects of labour income tax τ_W on consumption and investment?

4. Suppose the government uses labour income tax to finance its spending and the capital depreciation rate is positive. Derive the steady-state equilibrium levels of $\{l^*, K^*, I^*, Y^*, C^*\}$.

Chapter 7

Fiscal Policy: Capital Income Tax

In this chapter, we conclude our analysis of fiscal policy in the neoclassical growth model. In Chapter 6, we considered a labour income tax. However, labour income is not the only source of income that is taxed by the government. In this chapter, we consider instead a capital income tax, which is another tax instrument that we commonly observe in reality.[1] In this case, we find that capital income tax is also contractionary by decreasing the accumulation of capital.

7.1. Household

The household's utility function is given by

$$U = \int_0^\infty e^{-\rho t}[\ln C_t + \beta \ln(L - l_t)]dt, \qquad (7.1)$$

where the parameter $\rho > 0$ is the household's discount rate and the parameter $\beta > 0$ determines the importance of leisure $L - l_t$ relative to consumption C_t in the utility function. l_t is the level of employment chosen by the household. The household elastically supplies l_t units of labour to earn a wage income W_t. Furthermore, the household

---

[1]We do not consider government bonds here. Barro (1974) provides a theoretical foundation for the Ricardian equivalence proposition and shows that "shifts between debt and tax finance for a given amount of public expenditure would have no first-order effect". See also Romer (2018, Chapter 13).

accumulates capital K_t and rents it to the representative firm to earn an after-tax capital-rental income $(1 - \tau_R)R_t$, where $\tau_R > 0$ is the tax rate on capital income. The asset-accumulation equation is

$$\dot{K}_t = (1 - \tau_R)R_t K_t + W_t l_t - C_t - T_t, \tag{7.2}$$

where the capital depreciation rate is zero and T_t is a lump-sum tax.

7.2. Government

The government collects tax revenue to pay for government spending G_t. The balanced budget condition is $G_t = T_t + \tau_R R_t K_t$. We define the ratio of government spending to output as $\gamma \equiv G_t/Y_t$. We are interested in the effects of changes in the capital tax rate τ_R on other macroeconomic variables. In Chapter 5, we saw that changes in G_t cause an income effect on the household. To separate this income effect from our analysis, we assume that changes in the capital tax rate τ_R are balanced by changes in the lump-sum tax T_t while the government-spending ratio γ does not change.

7.3. Hamiltonian

The Hamiltonian function of the household is given by

$$H_t = \ln C_t + \beta \ln(L - l_t) + \lambda_t[(1 - \tau_R)R_t K_t + W_t l_t - C_t - T_t]. \tag{7.3}$$

The first-order conditions include

$$\frac{\partial H_t}{\partial l_t} = -\frac{\beta}{L - l_t} + \lambda_t W_t = 0, \tag{7.4}$$

$$\frac{\partial H_t}{\partial C_t} = \frac{1}{C_t} - \lambda_t = 0, \tag{7.5}$$

$$\frac{\partial H_t}{\partial K_t} = \lambda_t(1 - \tau_R)R_t = \lambda_t \rho - \dot{\lambda}_t. \tag{7.6}$$

Recall that K_t is a state variable (i.e., a variable that accumulates over time), so we have to set $\partial H_t/\partial K_t = \lambda_t \rho - \dot{\lambda}_t$. Combining (7.4) and (7.5) yields the labour supply curve l_t^s given by

$$l_t^s = L - \frac{\beta C_t}{W_t}, \tag{7.7}$$

which is increasing in the wage rate W_t (i.e., a substitution effect) and decreasing in consumption C_t (i.e., an income effect). Taking the log of (7.5) and substituting it into (7.6) yields the optimal consumption path:

$$\frac{\dot{C_t}}{C_t} = (1 - \tau_R)R_t - \rho, \tag{7.8}$$

which now depends on the after-tax rental price $(1 - \tau_R)R_t$.

7.4.   Firm

The firm's optimisation problem is the same as before. There is a representative firm in the economy, and this firm hires labour and rents capital from the household to produce output using the following production function:

$$Y_t = AK_t^\alpha l_t^{1-\alpha}, \tag{7.9}$$

where the parameter $\alpha \in (0,1)$ is the degree of capital intensity in production and A is the exogenous level of technology. The profit function Π_t is

$$\Pi_t = Y_t - R_t K_t - W_t l_t, \tag{7.10}$$

where we have implicitly chosen Y_t as the numeraire (i.e., the price of Y_t is normalised to unity). Differentiating (7.10) with respect to K_t and l_t yields

$$\frac{\partial \Pi_t}{\partial K_t} = \frac{\partial Y_t}{\partial K_t} - R_t = \alpha A \left(\frac{l_t}{K_t} \right)^{1-\alpha} - R_t = 0, \tag{7.11}$$

$$\frac{\partial \Pi_t}{\partial l_t} = \frac{\partial Y_t}{\partial l_t} - W_t = (1 - \alpha)A \left(\frac{K_t}{l_t} \right)^{\alpha} - W_t = 0. \tag{7.12}$$

These two equations are the demand functions for K_t and l_t. In summary, the demand functions for K_t and l_t are also the same as before.

7.5.   Long-Run Effects of Capital Income Tax

Equation (7.8) shows that capital income tax affects the household's optimal consumption path, which in turn determines the supply of capital. However, because the short-run capital supply curve is perfectly inelastic, capital income tax has no effect on the equilibrium level of capital at the moment when the tax rate τ_R changes. Therefore, we focus on the long-run effects of capital income tax in our analysis.[2]

In the long run, the level of capital fully adjusts to its steady-state equilibrium level. Recall that the optimal consumption path is given by

$$\frac{\dot{C}_t}{C_t} = (1 - \tau_R)R_t - \rho. \tag{7.13}$$

In the steady state, we have $\dot{C}_t = 0$. Therefore, the long-run supply curve of capital is perfectly elastic and given by

$$R_t = \frac{\rho}{1 - \tau_R}, \tag{7.14}$$

whereas the labour supply curve is

$$W_t = \frac{\beta C_t}{L - l_t}. \tag{7.15}$$

As for the demand curves of capital and labour, they are given by

$$R_t = \alpha A \left(\frac{l_t}{K_t}\right)^{1-\alpha} = \alpha \frac{Y_t}{K_t}, \tag{7.16}$$

$$W_t = (1 - \alpha)A \left(\frac{K_t}{l_t}\right)^{\alpha} = (1 - \alpha)\frac{Y_t}{l_t}. \tag{7.17}$$

---

[2]It can be shown that consumption jumps up at the moment when the tax rate τ_R increases. As a result, the labour supply curve shifts to the left, reducing the equilibrium levels of labour and output in the short run. Then, consumption gradually decreases towards a lower steady-state equilibrium level, shifting the labour supply curve to the right in the long run as we show in Figure 7.1.

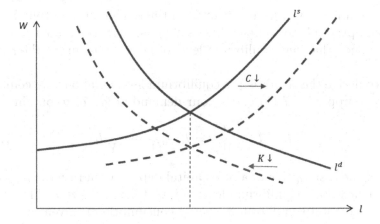

Figure 7.1. Labour market in the long run.

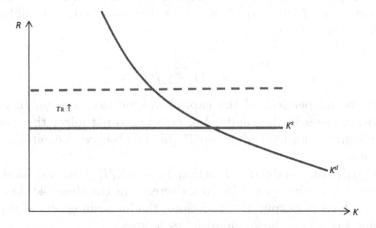

Figure 7.2. Capital market in the long run.

An increase in the capital income tax rate τ_R reduces the after-tax capital rental price and causes the household to accumulate less capital. Graphically, it shifts the capital supply upwards; as a result, the equilibrium level of capital K decreases in the capital market; see Figure 7.2. In the labour market, the decrease in the level of capital shifts the labour demand curve to the left. However, as can be seen from Figure 7.1, the labour supply curve shifts to the right (due to a negative income effect from the reduction in output Y and consumption C) to completely offset the shift in the labour demand curve such that the equilibrium level of labour remains at the initial level.[3]

To derive the steady-state equilibrium level of labour, we combine labour supply in (7.15) and labour demand in (7.17) to obtain

$$l_t = L - \frac{\beta C_t}{W_t} = L - \frac{\beta C_t}{(1-\alpha)Y_t} l_t. \tag{7.18}$$

Given the assumption of a zero capital depreciation rate (i.e., $\delta = 0$), the steady-state equilibrium level of investment I^* is zero. Therefore, the steady-state equilibrium level of consumption is given by

$$C^* = Y^* - G^* = (1 - \gamma)Y^*, \tag{7.19}$$

which is proportional to the steady-state equilibrium level of output. Substituting (7.19) into (7.18) yields the steady-state equilibrium level of labour l^* given by

$$l^* = \frac{L}{1 + \beta(1-\gamma)/(1-\alpha)}, \tag{7.20}$$

which is independent of the capital income tax rate τ_R. In other words, changes in the capital tax rate τ_R do not affect the steady-state equilibrium level of labour l^* (in the absence of capital depreciation).

Finally, the production function $Y_t = AK_t^\alpha l_t^{1-\alpha}$ implies that the decrease in capital gives rise to a decrease in the steady-state equilibrium level of output Y^*. Therefore, the long-run effects of capital income tax τ_R can be summarised as follows:

Long-run effects of an increase in τ_R				
Y	K	R	l	W
decrease	decrease	increase	no change	decrease

---

[3]This result is due to the zero capital depreciation rate; see Exercise 1 at the end of this chapter.

7.6. Government Spending Financed by Capital Income Tax

What happens when the government uses capital income tax to finance its spending? In this case, we eliminate lump-sum tax T_t and modify the balanced budget condition as $G_t = \tau_R R_t K_t$, which can be re-expressed as

$$\gamma = \alpha \tau_R, \tag{7.21}$$

using $G_t = \gamma Y_t$ and $R_t K_t = \alpha Y_t$. In other words, whenever the government increases spending γ, it has to raise the capital income tax rate according to $\tau_R = \gamma/\alpha$. Given that the capital income tax rate τ_R does not appear in (7.20), an increase in government spending γ increases the steady-state equilibrium level of labour as in Chapter 5. However, the resulting increase in the capital income tax rate τ_R leads to a decrease in the steady-state equilibrium level of capital as in Figure 7.2. Therefore, when government spending is financed by capital income tax, its overall effect on the steady-state equilibrium level of output is ambiguous.

7.7. Summary

In this chapter, we explore the long-run effects of permanent changes in the capital income tax rate in the neoclassical growth model with elastic labour supply. We find that an increase in the capital income tax rate causes the household to accumulate less capital and reduces the steady-state equilibrium level of capital, which in turn has a general-equilibrium effect on the labour market by shifting the labour demand curve to the left and by depressing the wage rate and the equilibrium level of labour. The decrease in the levels of capital and output reduces the level of consumption and gives rise to an income effect, which shifts the labour supply curve to the right. As a result, the wage rate decreases by a larger amount and the equilibrium level of labour may return to the initial level (depending on the capital depreciation rate).[4] In summary, an increase in the capital income tax

---

[4]See Exercise 1 at the end of this chapter.

rate has a contractionary effect on the macroeconomy by decreasing the wage rate and the levels of output, capital and generally labour but raises the pre-tax rental price of capital such that the after-tax rental price remains unchanged in the long run.

7.8.   Exercises

1. Consider a positive capital depreciation rate $\delta > 0$. In this case, the asset-accumulation equation becomes

$$\dot{K}_t = [(1 - \tau_R)R_t - \delta]K_t + W_t l_t - C_t - T_t. \qquad (7.22)$$

   Show that the optimal consumption path is given by

$$\frac{\dot{C}_t}{C_t} = (1 - \tau_R)R_t - \delta - \rho, \qquad (7.23)$$

   and that the steady-state equilibrium level of labour l^* is given by

$$l^* = \frac{L}{1 + \frac{\beta}{1-\alpha}\left[1 - \gamma - \frac{\alpha\delta}{\rho+\delta}(1 - \tau_R)\right]}. \qquad (7.24)$$

   Under a positive capital depreciation rate $\delta > 0$, although the labour supply curve shifts to the right as in Figure 7.1, it only partly offsets the shift in the labour demand curve such that the equilibrium level of labour l^* becomes decreasing in τ_R for a given γ.[5]

2. Derive the steady-state equilibrium levels of capital K^* and output Y^*.

3. What are the long-run effects of capital income tax τ_R on consumption and investment?

4. Suppose the government uses capital income tax to finance its spending and the capital depreciation rate is positive. Derive the steady-state equilibrium levels of $\{l^*, K^*, I^*, Y^*, C^*\}$.

---

[5]Substituting $\tau_R = \gamma/\alpha$ into (7.24), one can show that l^* continues to be increasing in γ as in Section 7.6 unless $\rho \to 0$.

Chapter 8

Monetary Policy in the New Keynesian Model

In this chapter, we consider monetary policy. Recall that in the neoclassical growth model, prices are fully flexible. In this case, changes in the level of money supply do not have any effect on real variables (i.e., the neutrality of money). Therefore, we need to introduce sticky prices into our model.[1] However, before we can consider sticky prices, we need to first develop a model in which firms have price-setting power. In other words, firms need to have the power to set their prices before they can decide whether or not to change their prices. Consequently, we need to convert the market structure from perfect competition to monopolistic competition.[2] In summary, we develop a New Keynesian model and find that increasing the money supply has an expansionary effect on the macroeconomy in the short run by increasing the demand for goods.[3]

---

[1]In the 1990s, economists started to introduce sticky prices into the RBC model. This combination of neoclassical economics and Keynesian macroeconomics is known as the new neoclassical synthesis; see e.g., Kimball (1995) for an early study.

[2]The model of monopolistic competition was developed by Dixit and Stiglitz (1977).

[3]See Gali (2015) and Romer (2018, Chapters 6 and 7) for a textbook treatment of the New Keynesian model.

8.1. A Simple New Keynesian Model

Given the complexity of the firm side, we keep the household side as simple as possible. Specifically, the household has an upward-sloping labour supply curve and a perfectly inelastic capital supply curve in the short run. We focus our analysis on the short run because sticky prices are a short-run phenomenon and monetary policy only has short-run effects. In the long run, prices become fully flexible, and the effects of monetary policy become neutral.

On the firm side, we need to distinguish between competitive firms that produce a final good and monopolistic firms that produce intermediate goods. There are N monopolistic firms that are indexed by $i \in [1, N]$ and sell differentiated intermediate goods y_i. The production function of monopolistic firm i is given by

$$y_i = AK_i^\alpha l_i^{1-\alpha}, \tag{8.1}$$

where $\alpha \in (0, 1)$ and $\{K_i, l_i\}$ are capital and labour employed by firm i. There is also a representative firm that produces final output Y by combining the differentiated intermediate goods using the following production function:

$$Y = \left(\sum_{i=1}^{N} y_i^\varepsilon \right)^{1/\varepsilon}, \tag{8.2}$$

which is known as a constant elasticity of substitution (CES) aggregator in which the parameter $\varepsilon \in (0, 1)$ determines the substitution elasticity $1/(1 - \varepsilon)$ between the differentiated intermediate goods. As ε approaches unity, the substitution elasticity $1/(1 - \varepsilon)$ goes to infinity, in which case the intermediate goods become perfect substitutes. In other words, the degree of substitutability between products is increasing in ε. The less substitutable the products are (i.e., a smaller ε), the more market power the monopolistic firms have.

8.2. Final Output

A representative firm produces final good, and the profit function Π is

$$\Pi = PY - \sum_{i=1}^{N} p_i y_i = P \left(\sum_{i=1}^{N} y_i^\varepsilon \right)^{1/\varepsilon} - \sum_{i=1}^{N} p_i y_i, \tag{8.3}$$

where P is the price of final good Y and p_i is the price of intermediate good y_i. The market structure in this sector is perfectly competitive, and the firm takes the prices as given. The first-order condition with respect to y_i is

$$\frac{\partial \Pi}{\partial y_i} = \frac{1}{\varepsilon} P \left(\sum_{i=1}^{N} y_i^{\varepsilon} \right)^{\frac{1-\varepsilon}{\varepsilon}} \varepsilon y_i^{\varepsilon-1} - p_i = 0, \tag{8.4}$$

which can be expressed as

$$p_i = PY^{1-\varepsilon} y_i^{\varepsilon-1} \Leftrightarrow y_i^d = \left(\frac{P}{p_i} \right)^{1/(1-\varepsilon)} Y. \tag{8.5}$$

This is the demand function y_i^d, in which the demand elasticity is $1/(1-\varepsilon)$. As ε approaches unity, the demand elasticity $1/(1-\varepsilon)$ goes to infinity, in which case the demand curve for y_i becomes perfectly elastic.

8.3. Intermediate Goods

A monopolistic firm produces intermediate product i. The profit function π_i is given by

$$\pi_i = p_i y_i - Wl_i - RK_i. \tag{8.6}$$

Here, we make the following assumption to simplify our analysis: the level of capital supplied to each firm is fixed in the short run. Under this assumption, firm i can only change its labour input whenever y_i changes in the short run.[4] The market structure in this sector is monopolistically competitive, so that the firm has a price-setting power. In other words, the firm sets its own price p_i, instead of taking it as given.

---

[4]If both capital and labour inputs can adjust, then we need to first perform cost minimisation to derive the marginal cost function before deriving the profit-maximising price; see the exercises at the end of this chapter.

Substituting the demand function in (8.5) into the profit function in (8.6) yields

$$\pi_i = PY^{1-\varepsilon} y_i^{\varepsilon} - Wl_i - RK_i, \tag{8.7}$$

where $\{W, R\}$ are the wage rate and the capital rental price as before. Differentiating (8.7) with respect to l_i yields

$$\frac{\partial \pi_i}{\partial l_i} = \underbrace{\varepsilon PY^{1-\varepsilon} y_i^{\varepsilon-1}}_{=p_i} \frac{\partial y_i}{\partial l_i} - W = 0, \tag{8.8}$$

which can be re-expressed as firm i's labour demand:

$$W = \varepsilon p_i MPL_i \Leftrightarrow l_i^d = \frac{\varepsilon(1-\alpha)p_i y_i}{W}, \tag{8.9}$$

where $\varepsilon < 1$.[5] In other words, a profit-maximising monopolistic firm would set its value of marginal product of labour above the wage rate (i.e., $W < p_i MPL_i$).

Equation (8.9) can also be re-expressed as

$$p_i = \frac{1}{\varepsilon} \frac{W}{MPL_i} = \frac{1}{\varepsilon} MC_i, \tag{8.10}$$

where W/MPL_i is the marginal cost MC_i of production. Given that $\varepsilon < 1$, the monopolistic price is above the marginal cost of production (i.e., $p_i > MC_i$). The markup ratio $1/\varepsilon > 1$ implies that the monopolistic firm makes a positive profit.

The positive monopolistic profit enables the firm to allow its price to temporarily deviate from its profit-maximising level without making a loss. For example, (8.10) shows that when the wage rate W increases, the firm would want to raise its price p_i to maximise profit. However, there may be some frictions (e.g., a menu cost) that prevent an immediate price adjustment. We summarise these frictions as sticky prices. When prices are sticky, monopolistic firms may not be able to maximise profit, but they would continue production so long as $p_i > MC_i$.

---

[5]Therefore, aggregate labour demand $\sum_{i=1}^{N} l_i^d = \varepsilon(1-\alpha)PY/W$ is decreasing in the real wage rate W/P.

8.4. Short-Run Effects of Monetary Policy

In this section, we explore the short-run effects of monetary policy. We define the short run as the duration in which the prices of firms do not change. Recall that the demand function y_i^d is given by

$$y_i^d = \left(\frac{P}{p_i}\right)^{1/(1-\varepsilon)} Y, \tag{8.11}$$

which is decreasing in the relative price p_i/P and increasing in aggregate output Y. To relate aggregate output to the level of money supply in the economy, we introduce the quantity theory of money given by

$$MV = PY, \tag{8.12}$$

where M is the level of money supply and V is the velocity of money in the economy. For simplicity, we set $V = 1$. Substituting (8.12) into (8.11) yields

$$y_i^d = \left(\frac{P}{p_i}\right)^{1/(1-\varepsilon)} \frac{M}{P}, \tag{8.13}$$

which relates the demand function y_i^d to the level of money supply M.

Given the assumption of sticky prices p_i, the aggregate price level P is also fixed in the short run.[6] Therefore, an increase in the level of money supply M would increase the demand y_i^d for product $i \in [1, N]$ by increasing aggregate output Y. Suppose the level of money supply M increases by a small amount given by $\Delta M > 0$. Then, the increase in the demand y_i^d is

$$\Delta y_i^d = \left(\frac{P}{p_i}\right)^{1/(1-\varepsilon)} \frac{\Delta M}{P}. \tag{8.14}$$

To satisfy the increased demand for its product, firm $i \in [1, N]$ needs to employ more labour, and the increase in the labour demand l_i^d is

$$\Delta l_i^d = \frac{\Delta y_i^d}{MPL_i} = \frac{1}{(1-\alpha)A(K_i/l_i)^\alpha} \left(\frac{P}{p_i}\right)^{1/(1-\varepsilon)} \frac{\Delta M}{P}, \tag{8.15}$$

---

[6]It can be shown that $P = [\sum_{i=1}^{N} p_i^{\varepsilon/(\varepsilon-1)}]^{(\varepsilon-1)/\varepsilon}$.

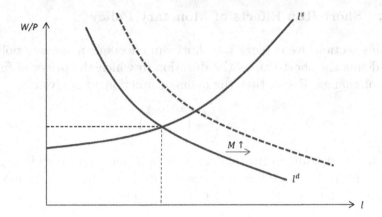

Figure 8.1.   Labour market in the short run.

where we have used the definition of the marginal product of labour $MPL_i \equiv \Delta y_i / \Delta l_i$. Given that all firms $i \in [1, N]$ demand more labour, aggregate labour demand increases by $\sum_{i=1}^{N} \Delta l_i^d$. Graphically, the labour demand curve shifts to the right. In the labour market, the equilibrium level of labour l and the real wage rate W/P increase; see Figure 8.1. Therefore, the short-run effects of an increase in money supply M can be summarised as follows:

Short-run effects of an increase in M			
Y	l	W/P	W
increase	increase	increase	increase

8.5.   Long-Run Effects of Monetary Policy

An increase in the level of money supply has an expansionary effect on the economy, but only in the short run. When prices become fully flexible in the long run, the price level P increases by the same proportion as the level of money supply M. Then, the expansionary effect disappears, and the real variables $\{Y, l, W/P\}$ return to their initial levels. Therefore, in the long run, an increase in the level of money supply M only causes the nominal variables $\{P, W, R\}$ to increase by the same proportion without affecting the real variables. This result is known as the neutrality of money and the classical dichotomy.

8.6. Summary

In this chapter, we explore the effects of monetary policy in a New Keynesian model. To allow for sticky prices, we consider a monopolistically competitive product market in which monopolistic firms have price-setting power. This price-setting power enables each firm to price its differentiated product above the marginal cost of production. The presence of this markup allows the firm to let its price temporarily deviate from the profit-maximising level while still making a positive monopolistic profit. When prices are sticky in the short run, an increase in the level of money supply increases the demand for goods, which in turn increases the demand for factor inputs (e.g., labour). In this case, an increase in the level of money supply has an expansionary effect on the economy by increasing the level of output, the level of labour, the real wage rate and the nominal wage rate. However, this expansionary effect disappears when prices fully adjust in the long run, in which case the higher level of money supply increases the price level and the nominal wage rate without affecting the level of output, the level of labour and the real wage rate.

8.7. Exercises

1. Suppose all the monopolistic firms $i \in [1, N]$ can now adjust their capital input K_i in addition to labour input l_i when y_i changes in the short run. Show that the marginal cost of producing y_i is given by[7]

$$MC_i = \frac{1}{A} \left(\frac{R}{\alpha} \right)^\alpha \left(\frac{W}{1 - \alpha} \right)^{1-\alpha}. \qquad (8.16)$$

2. Given (8.16), show that the profit-maximising price $p_i = MC_i/\varepsilon$ continues to hold. Also, derive the amount of monopolistic profit π_i and show that $\pi_i \to 0$ as $\varepsilon \to 1$. Explain the intuition.
3. Suppose monopolistic firms can adjust their capital input K_i in addition to labour input l_i when y_i changes in the short run. How does an increase in the level of money supply affect the capital market in the short run?

---

[7]Hint: Minimise $TC_i \equiv Wl_i + RK_i$ subject to $y_i = AK_i^\alpha l_i^{1-\alpha} \geq Q$, where Q is an arbitrary number. Then, $MC_i = \partial TC_i/\partial Q$.

Chapter 9

The Solow Growth Model

The level of income varies drastically across countries with the richest country being more than 100 times richer than the poorest country in the world. According to the International Monetary Fund, GDP (at purchasing power parity) per capita across countries ranges from about $700 in the Central African Republic to about $130,000 in Qatar in 2018. Suppose we consider two hypothetical countries that have a real GDP per capita of $1,000 in the early 19th century. If one country grows at 1% per year, then after two centuries this country would have a real GDP per capita of about $7,300, which is roughly the income level of India and Vietnam. If the other country grows at 2% per year, then after two centuries this country would have a real GDP per capita of about $52,500, which is roughly the income level of Australia and Germany. Therefore, a small difference in the growth rates accumulated over a long period of time can lead to very large income differences. However, what determines the rate of economic growth?

In this chapter, we begin our analysis of economic growth.[1] A seminal model of economic growth is the Solow growth model.[2] We will review the useful insights that one can obtain from this model

---

[1]Other textbook treatments of economic growth include Aghion and Howitt (2009) and Jones and Vollrath (2013) at the advanced undergraduate level and Acemoglu (2009), Barro and Sala-i-Martin (2003), Galor (2011) and Romer (2018, chapters 1–4) at the postgraduate level.

[2]The Solow growth model was developed by Solow (1956), who received the Nobel Memorial Prize in Economics in 1987 partly for this contribution. Swan

and also discuss its limitations. In summary, the Solow model shows that capital accumulation cannot sustain long-run economic growth, which requires technological progress; however, the model treats technological progress as exogenous and does not inform us on its determinants. The Solow model consists of the following components: an aggregate production function; an accumulation equation for capital; and an exogenous saving rate.

9.1. The Solow Model Without Technological Progress

Output Y_t at time t is produced by the Cobb–Douglas production function:

$$Y_t = AK_t^\alpha L_t^{1-\alpha}, \tag{9.1}$$

where the parameter $\alpha \in (0, 1)$ is the degree of capital intensity in production and A is the exogenous level of technology. K_t is the stock of capital that has been accumulated as of time t. L_t is the size of the labour force in the economy at time t. For simplicity, we assume that the size of the labour force is constant, and we normalise L_t to unity so that other variables can be interpreted as per capita variables (e.g., output per capita).

The second key equation in this model is the accumulation equation for capital given by

$$\dot{K}_t = I_t - \delta K_t, \tag{9.2}$$

where the parameter $\delta > 0$ is the depreciation rate of capital, $\dot{K}_t \equiv \partial K_t/\partial t$ denotes the change in the stock of capital with respect to time t, and I_t is capital investment. In this closed economy without

---

(1956) also developed a similar growth model; therefore, the Solow model is often referred to as the Solow–Swan model.

a government sector, the national income account is simply

$$Y_t = C_t + I_t, \tag{9.3}$$

where C_t is consumption in the economy at time t. The Solow growth model is quite simple because it assumes an exogenous saving (or investment) rate denoted by s. In other words,

$$s \equiv \frac{I_t}{Y_t} = 1 - \frac{C_t}{Y_t}. \tag{9.4}$$

To solve this model, we substitute (9.1) and (9.4) into (9.2) to obtain

$$\dot{K}_t = sAK_t^\alpha - \delta K_t, \tag{9.5}$$

where we have used $L_t = 1$. Equation (9.5) is a one-dimensional differential equation in K_t. Imposing $\dot{K}_t = 0$ on (9.5) yields the steady-state level of capital given by

$$K^* = \left(\frac{sA}{\delta} \right)^{1/(1-\alpha)}. \tag{9.6}$$

Equation (9.5) implies that whenever $K_t < K^*$, K_t would increase over time until it reaches K^*; see Figure 9.1. Similarly, whenever, $K_t > K^*$, K_t would decrease over time until it reaches K^*. Equation (9.6) shows that K^* is increasing in the saving rate s and the level of technology A but decreasing in the depreciation rate δ.

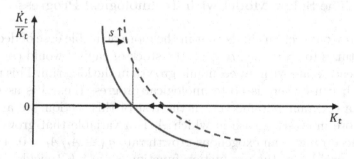

Figure 9.1. Phase diagram.

When the level of capital converges to its steady state K^*, the level of output also reaches its steady-state level given by $Y^* = A(K^*)^\alpha$. Although Y^* is increasing in the saving rate s, the level of output is stationary in the long run. Why doesn't the output keep growing in the long run? To answer this question, we rewrite (9.5) to derive an expression for the growth rate of capital.

$$\frac{\dot{K}_t}{K_t} = \frac{sA}{K_t^{1-\alpha}} - \delta. \tag{9.7}$$

This equation shows that as K_t increases, the growth rate of capital $\dot{K}_t/K_t$ decreases and eventually converges to a long-run value of zero. An increase in the saving rate s would increase the growth rate of capital in the short run, but the growth rate of capital always converges to zero in the long run; see Figure 9.1.

The reason behind this convergence process is decreasing returns to scale (i.e., $\alpha < 1$) with respect to capital in the production function. As capital increases, output increases; however, the additional output that the additional capital produces is decreasing. This diminishing marginal product of capital implies that the additional investment created by the additional output is also decreasing. Given that capital accumulation requires capital investment, the growth rate of capital decreases and converges to zero. If the production function instead features constant returns to scale (i.e., $\alpha = 1$), then the long-run growth rate of capital would be $\dot{K}_t/K_t = sA - \delta$, which remains positive so long as $sA > \delta$.

9.2.   The Solow Model with Technological Progress

The previous section shows that in the more plausible case of decreasing returns to scale (i.e., $\alpha < 1$), the stock of capital would converge to a steady state without economic growth in the long run. This result arises because there is no technological progress (i.e., A is assumed to be a constant parameter). In the rest of this section, we analyse the more interesting case in which A_t is a variable that grows over time according to an exogenous growth rate $g_A \equiv \dot{A}_t/A_t > 0$. Taking the natural log of the production function $Y_t = A_t K_t^\alpha$ yields

$$\ln Y_t = \ln A_t + \alpha \ln K_t. \tag{9.8}$$

Differentiating this equation with respect to t yields[3]

$$\frac{\dot{Y}_t}{Y_t} = \frac{\dot{A}_t}{A_t} + \alpha \frac{\dot{K}_t}{K_t},\qquad(9.9)$$

where $\dot{A}_t/A_t = g_A$ is an exogenous parameter.

Substituting (9.4) into (9.2) and dividing by K_t yields

$$\frac{\dot{K}_t}{K_t} = s\frac{Y_t}{K_t} - \delta.\qquad(9.10)$$

In the long run, the economy is on a balanced growth path (BGP) along which each variable grows at a constant rate.[4] Because $\dot{K}_t/K_t$ is constant on the BGP, Y_t/K_t is also constant implying that output Y_t and capital K_t grow at the same rate on the BGP. Using this information and (9.9), we can now derive the long-run growth rate of output Y_t and capital K_t on the BGP given by

$$\frac{\dot{Y}_t}{Y_t} = \frac{\dot{K}_t}{K_t} = \frac{g_A}{1 - \alpha}.\qquad(9.11)$$

This equation reveals a key insight of the Solow model: economic growth in the long run is driven by technological progress.

Where does technological progress come from? Unfortunately, the Solow model cannot be used to analyse this question because technological progress is exogenous in the model. In other words, although the Solow model allows us to explore the relative importance of technological progress and capital accumulation, which Acemoglu (2009) refers to as proximate causes of economic growth, it does not allow us to explore the fundamental causes of economic growth. In Chapter 13, we study the Romer model in which the technology growth rate g_A is endogenously determined by R&D and innovation in the market economy, which allows us to explore how fundamental causes, such as culture (the household's preference) and institutions (intellectual property rights), affect economic growth via technological progress. Similarly, the Solow model features an exogenous saving rate, which determines capital accumulation as a proximate cause of growth;

---

[3]Recall that $\frac{\partial \ln Y_t}{\partial t} = \frac{1}{Y_t}\frac{\partial Y_t}{\partial t} = \frac{\dot{Y}_t}{Y_t}$.

[4]Because this constant growth rate can be zero, a steady state is a special case of a balanced growth path.

however, it cannot be used to analyse the question on why the saving rate differs across countries. In Chapter 10, we introduce a utility-maximising household, which chooses consumption and saving, to explore the fundamental determinants of the saving rate.

9.3. Summary

In this chapter, we review the Solow growth model. In the absence of technological progress, the economy always converges to a steady state, in which the long-run levels of capital and output are stationary and increasing in the saving rate and the level of technology but decreasing in the depreciation rate of capital. The absence of long-run economic growth is due to the decreasing returns to scale with respect to capital in the production function. Therefore, unless capital exhibits constant returns to scale in production, capital accumulation alone cannot sustain economic growth in the long run without technological progress. In the presence of technological progress, the long-run growth rate of output and capital is determined by the growth rate of technology, which however is exogenous in the Solow growth model. Therefore, one cannot use the Solow growth model to explore the determinants of technological progress.

9.4. Exercises

1. Use (9.7) and the phase diagram in Figure 9.1 to show the effects of (a) a one-time increase in the level of technology A and (b) a continuous increase in the level of technology A.
2. Derive the steady-state level of consumption. Show that setting the saving rate to $s = \alpha$ maximises the steady-state level of consumption.
3. Suppose $L_t = L$. Derive the steady-state levels of capital per capita and output per capita.
4. Suppose the growth rate of labour is $\dot{L}_t/L_t = n$. Derive the steady-state levels of capital per capita and output per capita in the Solow model.

5. Suppose the growth rate of labour is $\dot{L}_t/L_t = n$ and the growth rate of technology is $\dot{A}_t/A_t = g_A$. What is the long-run growth rate of output per capita in the Solow model?

6. Consider an extension of the Solow growth model with human capital accumulation. The production function is $Y_t = AK_t^\alpha H_t^{1-\alpha}$, where H_t is human capital. The level of technology A is constant. The accumulation equation of physical capital K_t is $\dot{K}_t = s_K Y_t - \delta K_t$, where $s_K \in (0, 1)$ is the investment rate of K_t and $\delta > 0$ is the depreciation rate of K_t. The accumulation equation of human capital H_t is $\dot{H}_t = s_H Y_t - \delta H_t$, where $s_K \in (0, 1)$ is the investment rate of H_t and $\delta > 0$ is also the depreciation rate of H_t. What is the long-run growth rate of output Y_t?

Chapter 10

The Ramsey Model

In this chapter, we continue our analysis of economic growth by developing the Ramsey model,[1] which can be viewed as a generalisation of the Solow growth model. The Solow model assumes an exogenous saving rate, whereas the Ramsey model features a representative household which chooses the saving rate optimally. As we saw in the Solow model, although the saving rate does not affect the long-run growth rate, it affects the levels of capital and output. Therefore, the Ramsey model allows us to explore the question on why the saving rate differs across countries, which explains some of the variation in the level of income across countries. In summary, we find that the saving rate is determined by the household's discount rate, the degree of capital intensity in production and the depreciation rate of capital but independent of the level of technology. Aside from the endogenous saving rate, the rest of the Ramsey model is the same as the Solow model.

10.1. Household

In the Ramsey model, there is a representative household, which has a utility function u_t at time t. As in the neoclassical growth model,

---

[1] The Ramsey model was developed by Ramsey (1928) and further extended by Cass (1965) and Koopmans (1965), so it is often referred to as the Ramsey–Cass–Koopmans model.

we consider a log utility function:

$$u_t = \ln C_t, \tag{10.1}$$

which depends on consumption C_t at time t. Given the discount rate $\rho > 0$, the lifetime utility function is given by

$$U = u_0 + \frac{u_1}{1 + \rho} + \frac{u_2}{(1 + \rho)^2} + \cdots = \sum_{t=0}^{\infty} \frac{u_t}{(1 + \rho)^t}, \tag{10.2}$$

where we assume that a lifetime is long enough to be approximated by infinity.[2] In this analysis, we will once again use the Hamiltonian to solve the household's dynamic optimisation problem in continuous time. Therefore, we need to rewrite (10.2) in continuous time using the integral as

$$U = \int_0^{\infty} e^{-\rho t} u_t dt = \int_0^{\infty} e^{-\rho t} \ln C_t dt, \tag{10.3}$$

where the continuous-time discount factor $e^{-\rho t}$ replaces the discrete-time discount factor $(1 + \rho)^{-t}$.

As in the Solow model, output Y_t at time t is produced by the Cobb-Douglas production function:

$$Y_t = AK_t^{\alpha} L_t^{1-\alpha}, \tag{10.4}$$

where the parameter $\alpha \in (0, 1)$ is the degree of capital intensity in production and A is the exogenous level of technology. K_t is the stock of capital that has been accumulated as of time t. L_t is the size of the labour force, which we normalise to unity. The accumulation equation for capital is

$$\dot{K}_t = I_t - \delta K_t, \tag{10.5}$$

where the parameter $\delta > 0$ is the depreciation rate of capital, and I_t is capital investment. In this closed economy without a government

---

[2] As t becomes very large, the discounting would make $u_t/(1+\rho)^t$ not to matter too much in the utility function U.

sector, the national income account is simply

$$Y_t = C_t + I_t. \tag{10.6}$$

Substituting (10.4) and (10.6) into (10.5) yields

$$\dot{K}_t = Y_t - C_t - \delta K_t = AK_t^\alpha - C_t - \delta K_t, \tag{10.7}$$

where we have set $L_t = 1$.

With the above information, we can now set up the dynamic optimisation problem faced by the representative household. The household chooses consumption C_t and accumulates capital K_t in order to maximise lifetime utility. Formally, the optimisation problem is

$$\max_{C_t} U = \int_0^\infty e^{-\rho t} \ln C_t dt, \tag{10.8}$$

subject to

$$\dot{K}_t = AK_t^\alpha - C_t - \delta K_t. \tag{10.9}$$

10.2. Hamiltonian

To solve the dynamic optimisation problem in (10.8) and (10.9), we use the Hamiltonian. We proceed as follows. First, we set up the Hamiltonian function. Then, we derive the first-order conditions. Finally, we use the first-order conditions to derive the steady-state levels of C_t and K_t. The Hamiltonian function is given by

$$H_t = \ln C_t + \lambda_t(AK_t^\alpha - C_t - \delta K_t). \tag{10.10}$$

The Hamiltonian consists of (a) the utility function $\ln C_t$ at time t, (b) the right-hand side of the capital-accumulation equation $AK_t^\alpha - C_t - \delta K_t$, and (c) a multiplier λ_t for the capital-accumulation equation.

Now, we derive the first-order conditions with respect to C_t and K_t. The first-order conditions include

$$\frac{\partial H_t}{\partial C_t} = \frac{1}{C_t} - \lambda_t = 0, \tag{10.11}$$

$$\frac{\partial H_t}{\partial K_t} = \lambda_t(\alpha AK_t^{\alpha-1} - \delta) = \lambda_t \rho - \dot{\lambda}_t. \tag{10.12}$$

Note that K_t is a state variable (i.e., a variable that accumulates over time), so we have to set $\partial H_t/\partial K_t = \lambda_t\rho - \dot{\lambda}_t$. From (10.11), we have $C_t = \lambda_t^{-1}$. Taking the log of this equation yields

$$\ln C_t = -\ln \lambda_t. \tag{10.13}$$

Differentiating it with respect to t yields

$$\frac{\dot{C}_t}{C_t} = -\frac{\dot{\lambda}_t}{\lambda_t}. \tag{10.14}$$

Substituting this equation into (10.12) yields

$$\frac{\dot{C}_t}{C_t} = -\frac{\dot{\lambda}_t}{\lambda_t} = \alpha AK_t^{\alpha-1} - \delta - \rho. \tag{10.15}$$

Equation (10.15) is the optimal path of consumption chosen by the household. The optimal path of consumption states that if the net return to capital (i.e., the marginal product of capital $\alpha AK_t^{\alpha-1}$ net of depreciation δ) is greater than the discount rate ρ, then the household should save more and consume less today. Because current consumption is relatively low, consumption must be increasing over time so that $\dot{C}_t > 0$. On the other hand, if the net return to capital is less than the discount rate, then the household should save less and consume more today. Because current consumption is relatively high, consumption must be decreasing over time so that $\dot{C}_t < 0$.

10.3. Steady State

In summary, the Ramsey model provides us with two differential equations:

$$\frac{\dot{C}_t}{C_t} = \alpha AK_t^{\alpha-1} - \delta - \rho, \tag{10.16}$$

$$\dot{K}_t = AK_t^{\alpha} - C_t - \delta K_t. \tag{10.17}$$

Now, we solve for the steady state.[3] In the steady state, $\dot{C}_t = 0$ and $\dot{K}_t = 0$. Imposing $\dot{C}_t = 0$ on the optimal consumption path

---

[3]One can use the phase diagram of (10.16) and (10.17) to show that the economy converges to this steady state.

in (10.16) yields the steady-state level of capital:

$$K^* = \left(\frac{\alpha A}{\rho + \delta}\right)^{1/(1-\alpha)}, \tag{10.18}$$

which is increasing in the level of technology A and decreasing in the discount rate ρ and the depreciation rate δ. Intuitively, a higher level of technology A increases the return to capital and encourages the household to accumulate more capital. In contrast, a higher discount rate ρ makes future consumption less attractive to the household, which then accumulates less capital. Finally, a higher depreciation rate δ also makes capital depreciate more rapidly, so that the level of accumulated capital becomes lower.

Imposing $\dot{K}_t = 0$ on the capital-accumulation equation in (10.17) yields the steady-state level of consumption:

$$C^* = A(K^*)^\alpha - \delta K^* = \frac{\rho + \delta(1-\alpha)}{\rho + \delta}\left(\frac{\alpha A}{\rho + \delta}\right)^{\alpha/(1-\alpha)} A. \tag{10.19}$$

Using the production function, we can also derive the steady-state level of output given by

$$Y^* = A(K^*)^\alpha = \left(\frac{\alpha A}{\rho + \delta}\right)^{\alpha/(1-\alpha)} A. \tag{10.20}$$

As for the steady-state level of investment, it is given by

$$I^* = Y^* - C^* = \delta K^* = \left(\frac{\alpha A}{\rho + \delta}\right)^{1/(1-\alpha)} \delta. \tag{10.21}$$

To derive the steady-state saving rate s^*, we use

$$s^* \equiv \frac{I^*}{Y^*} = \frac{\delta K^*}{A(K^*)^\alpha} = \frac{\alpha \delta}{\rho + \delta}, \tag{10.22}$$

which is increasing in the degree of capital intensity α and the depreciation rate δ but decreasing in the discount rate ρ. The intuition of these results can be explained as follows. If capital becomes more important in production (i.e., a larger α), then the household would save more to accumulate capital. A higher discount rate ρ makes future consumption less attractive to the household, which then saves less. As for the capital depreciation rate δ, it has two effects on the household's saving rate. First, it reduces the net return to capital and makes saving less attractive, which is captured by the δ in the denominator of s^*. Second, capital depreciation requires investment to replace the depreciated capital. This replacement effect, which is captured by the δ in the numerator of s^*, implies that a larger δ requires a higher saving rate s^*. Overall, the positive replacement effect of δ dominates unless $\rho \to 0$, in which case the two effects exactly offset each other.

Finally, we substitute $s^*/\delta = \alpha/(\rho + \delta)$ into (10.18) to obtain

$$K^* = \left(\frac{s^* A}{\delta}\right)^{1/(1-\alpha)}, \tag{10.23}$$

which is the same as K^* in (9.6) except that s is exogenous in the Solow model whereas s^* is endogenous in the Ramsey model.

10.4. Summary

In this chapter, we explore the Ramsey model, which generalises the Solow growth model by featuring an endogenous saving rate that is optimally chosen by a utility-maximising household. The Solow growth model shows that an increase in the exogenous saving rate gives rise to a higher growth rate in the short run and a higher level of output in the long run, which demonstrates the importance of capital accumulation as a proximate cause of economic growth. However, one cannot use the Solow growth model to explore the fundamental determinants of capital accumulation, which the Ramsey model allows us to do. In summary, we find that the steady-state saving rate is increasing in the degree of capital intensity and the depreciation rate of capital but decreasing in the discount rate, which reflects the preference of the representative household and captures a cultural trait. Therefore, cross-country variation in these determinants helps to explain some of the variation in income level across countries.

10.5. Exercises

1. Compare the steady-state saving rate from the Ramsey model to the consumption-maximising saving rate s in the Solow model.

Which one is higher? Under what condition would they be the same?

2. Suppose $L_t = L$. Derive the steady-state saving rate in the Ramsey model.

3. Consider the introduction of leisure to the household's utility function:

$$U = \int_0^\infty e^{-\rho t}[\ln C_t + \beta \ln(1 - l_t)]dt, \qquad (10.24)$$

where the parameter $\beta > 0$ determines the importance of leisure $1 - l_t$ in the utility function. In this case, the capital-accumulation equation becomes

$$\dot{K}_t = A K_t^\alpha l_t^{1-\alpha} - C_t - \delta K_t. \qquad (10.25)$$

Show that the steady-state level of labour l^* is given by

$$l^* = \frac{1}{1 + \frac{\beta}{1-\alpha}\left(1 - \frac{\alpha\delta}{\rho+\delta}\right)}. \qquad (10.26)$$

4. Suppose the growth rate of labour is $\dot{L}_t/L_t = n$. Derive the steady-state saving rate in the Ramsey model.

5. Suppose the growth rate of labour is $\dot{L}_t/L_t = n$ and the growth rate of technology is $\dot{A}_t/A_t = g_A$. Derive the steady-state saving rate and the long-run growth rate of output in the Ramsey model.

Chapter 11

The Ramsey Model with a Perfectly Competitive Market

In the previous chapter, we cover the Ramsey model, in which the representative household carries out the production of goods. However, this setting is unrealistic because goods are often produced by firms in the real world. In this chapter, we introduce a market economy to the Ramsey model, in which the representative household supplies labour and capital to a representative firm, which then uses these factor inputs to produce output and sells the output back to the household. As you can see, this familiar setting is basically the neoclassical growth model of Chapter 2. After deriving the equilibrium allocation of resources in the decentralised market economy, we can then compare it to the allocation in the centralised economy that is optimally chosen by the representative household as in Chapter 10. In summary, we find that the two sets of allocations are the same, implying that the market economy is efficient. In other words, the first fundamental theorem of welfare economics holds in this setting due to the absence of distortion in the market economy.

11.1. Household

In the Ramsey model, there is a representative household, which has the following lifetime utility function:

$$U = \int_0^\infty e^{-\rho t} \ln C_t dt, \qquad (11.1)$$

where the parameter $\rho > 0$ is the household's discount rate and C_t is the level of consumption at time t. The household inelastically supplies one unit of labour to earn a wage income W_t. Furthermore, it accumulates capital K_t and rents it to the representative firm to earn a capital-rental income R_t. If we normalise the price of output to unity, then the asset-accumulation equation is[1]

$$\dot{K}_t = R_t K_t + W_t - C_t - \delta K_t, \qquad (11.2)$$

where the parameter $\delta > 0$ is the depreciation rate of capital.

To solve this dynamic optimisation problem, we use the Hamiltonian. The Hamiltonian function is given by

$$H_t = \ln C_t + \lambda_t (R_t K_t + W_t - C_t - \delta K_t). \qquad (11.3)$$

The first-order conditions include

$$\frac{\partial H_t}{\partial C_t} = \frac{1}{C_t} - \lambda_t = 0, \qquad (11.4)$$

$$\frac{\partial H_t}{\partial K_t} = \lambda_t (R_t - \delta) = \lambda_t \rho - \dot{\lambda}_t. \qquad (11.5)$$

Recall once again that K_t is a state variable (i.e., a variable that accumulates over time). Taking the log of (11.4) yields

$$\ln C_t = -\ln \lambda_t. \qquad (11.6)$$

Differentiating it with respect to t yields

$$\frac{\dot{C}_t}{C_t} = -\frac{\dot{\lambda}_t}{\lambda_t}. \qquad (11.7)$$

Substituting this equation into (11.5) yields

$$\frac{\dot{C}_t}{C_t} = R_t - \delta - \rho, \qquad (11.8)$$

which is the optimal path of consumption chosen by the household.

---

[1]Here, we assume that one unit of output can be converted into one unit of consumption or one unit of capital.

11.2. Firm

We now consider the firm's optimisation problem. There is a representative firm in the economy, and this firm hires labour L_t and rents capital K_t from the household to produce output Y_t using the following production function:

$$Y_t = AK_t^\alpha L_t^{1-\alpha}, \tag{11.9}$$

where the parameter $\alpha \in (0,1)$ is the degree of capital intensity in production and A is the exogenous level of technology. The profit function Π_t is

$$\Pi_t = Y_t - R_t K_t - W_t L_t, \tag{11.10}$$

where we have chosen Y_t as the numeraire (i.e., the price of Y_t is normalised to unity). Differentiating (11.10) with respect to K_t and L_t yields

$$\frac{\partial \Pi_t}{\partial K_t} = \frac{\partial Y_t}{\partial K_t} - R_t = \alpha A K_t^{\alpha-1} L_t^{1-\alpha} - R_t = 0, \tag{11.11}$$

$$\frac{\partial \Pi_t}{\partial L_t} = \frac{\partial Y_t}{\partial L_t} - W_t = (1-\alpha) A K_t^{\alpha} L_t^{-\alpha} - W_t = 0. \tag{11.12}$$

These two equations are the demand functions for K_t and L_t.

11.3. Equilibrium

Substituting (11.11) into the consumption path in (11.8) yields

$$\frac{\dot{C}_t}{C_t} = \alpha A K_t^{\alpha-1} - \delta - \rho, \tag{11.13}$$

where we have set $L_t = 1$. Substituting (11.11) and (11.12) into (11.2) yields the capital-accumulation equation:

$$\dot{K}_t = \alpha A K_t^{\alpha} + (1-\alpha) A K_t^{\alpha} - C_t - \delta K_t = A K_t^{\alpha} - C_t - \delta K_t. \tag{11.14}$$

Equations (11.13) and (11.14) are two differential equations in C_t and K_t, and these two equations completely characterise the behaviour of the economy.

It is important to note that (11.13) and (11.14) are exactly the same as (10.16) and (10.17) in the Ramsey model in the previous chapter. Therefore, the decentralised market economy has the same allocation of resources as the centralised economy that is optimally chosen by the representative household. The reason is that the rental price R_t in the market economy is equal to the marginal product of capital $\alpha A K_t^{\alpha-1}$. This also implies that the decentralised economy has the same steady-state equilibrium allocations as the centralised economy. For example, the steady-state equilibrium level of capital is the same as before such that

$$K^* = \left(\frac{\alpha A}{\rho + \delta} \right)^{1/(1-\alpha)}, \qquad (11.15)$$

and the household's saving rate s^* is also the same as before such that

$$s^* \equiv \frac{I^*}{Y^*} = \frac{\delta K^*}{A(K^*)^\alpha} = \frac{\alpha \delta}{\rho + \delta}. \qquad (11.16)$$

This result is an example of the first fundamental theorem of welfare economics, which states that any competitive equilibrium leads to a Pareto efficient allocation of resources. This fundamental theorem holds because the decentralised economy is characterised by perfect competition in the production sector, so that $R_t = MPK_t = \alpha A K_t^{\alpha-1}$. In Chapter 12, we will consider another version of the Ramsey model with monopolistic competition under which the decentralised economy differs from the centralised economy (i.e., the decentralised economy exhibits market failure).

11.4. Summary

In this chapter, we introduce a market economy into the Ramsey model. Specifically, we consider a perfectly competitive product market. In this case, a representative firm demands factor inputs from the representative household and supplies output to the household. Therefore, the household and the firm interact in the labour market, the capital market and the product market. We find that the equilibrium allocation of resources in the market economy is the same as the socially optimal allocation in the centralised version of the Ramsey model in Chapter 10. In other words, due to the absence of distortion in the economy, the market equilibrium is efficient. Therefore, the first fundamental theorem of welfare economics holds in the Ramsey model with a perfectly competitive product market.

11.5. Exercises

1. Compare the steady-state saving rate from the competitive version of the Ramsey model to the consumption-maximising saving rate s in the Solow model. Which one is higher? Under what condition would they be the same?
2. Suppose $L_t = L$. Derive the steady-state saving rate in the competitive version of Ramsey model.
3. Consider the introduction of leisure to the household's utility function:

$$U = \int_0^\infty e^{-\rho t}[\ln C_t + \beta \ln(1 - l_t)]dt, \qquad (11.17)$$

where the parameter $\beta > 0$ determines the importance of leisure $1 - l_t$ in the utility function. In this case, the asset-accumulation equation becomes

$$\dot{K}_t = R_t K_t + W_t l_t - C_t - \delta K_t. \qquad (11.18)$$

Show that the steady-state equilibrium level of labour l^* is given by

$$l^* = \frac{1}{1 + \frac{\beta}{1-\alpha}\left(1 - \frac{\alpha\delta}{\rho+\delta}\right)}, \qquad (11.19)$$

which is the same as (10.26) in the centralised economy of the Ramsey model. Once again, due to the absence of market failure, the level of employment in the decentralised market economy is the same as the centralised allocation of labour that is optimally chosen by the representative household.

4. Suppose the growth rate of labour is $\dot{L}_t/L_t = n$. Derive the steady-state saving rate in the competitive version of the Ramsey model.
5. Suppose the growth rate of labour is $\dot{L}_t/L_t = n$ and the growth rate of technology is $\dot{A}_t/A_t = g_A$. Derive the steady-state saving rate and the long-run growth rate of output in the competitive version of the Ramsey model.

Chapter 12

The Ramsey Model
with a Monopolistically
Competitive Market

In this chapter, we will consider another form of market structure in the Ramsey model. Specifically, we consider monopolistic competition. In the model, there is a representative firm that produces the final good. Also, there are a number of firms that produce differentiated intermediate goods. Because each of these intermediate-good firms sells a differentiated product, it has market power and charges a markup over the marginal cost. This monopolistic distortion in turn causes the decentralised economy to have a different allocation of resources from the centralised economy. In other words, the first fundamental theorem of welfare economics does not hold in this setting due to the distortion of monopolistic competition, which in turn gives rise to market failure.

The model has the following components: (a) a representative household, (b) a representative firm that produces the final good, and (c) N monopolistic firms that produce differentiated intermediate goods.

12.1.   Household

The representative household has the following lifetime utility function:

$$U = \int_0^\infty e^{-\rho t} \ln C_t dt, \qquad (12.1)$$

where the parameter $\rho > 0$ is the household's discount rate and C_t is the level of consumption at time t. As usual, the household inelastically supplies one unit of labour to earn a wage income W_t. Furthermore, it accumulates capital K_t and rents it to firms to earn a capital-rental income R_t. The asset-accumulation equation is

$$\dot{K}_t = R_t K_t + W_t + \sum_{i=1}^{N} \pi_t(i) - C_t - \delta K_t, \qquad (12.2)$$

where the parameter $\delta > 0$ is the depreciation rate of capital. It is useful to note that each intermediate-good firm i generates monopolistic profit $\pi_t(i)$, which is transferred back to the household as it owns the firm. We have dealt with this dynamic optimisation problem many times now, so we will skip the steps and simply write down the result. The familiar consumption path is given by

$$\frac{\dot{C}_t}{C_t} = R_t - \delta - \rho, \qquad (12.3)$$

which determines the path of consumption chosen by the household.

12.2.   Final Good

There is a representative firm that produces the final good Y_t. This firm hires labour L_t and uses intermediate goods as inputs. The production function is different from before and given by

$$Y_t = L_t^{1-\alpha} \sum_{i=1}^{N} X_t^\alpha(i) = L_t^{1-\alpha} \left[X_t^\alpha(1) + X_t^\alpha(2) + \cdots + X_t^\alpha(N) \right],$$

$$(12.4)$$

where the parameter $\alpha \in (0, 1)$ determines the degree of labour intensity $1 - \alpha$ in production. In other words, there are N different intermediate goods $X_t(i)$ that are indexed by $i \in [1, N]$. The profit function for this final-good firm is

$$\Pi_t = Y_t - W_t L_t - \sum_{i=1}^{N} P_t(i) X_t(i), \qquad (12.5)$$

where we have implicitly chosen Y_t as the numeraire and $P_t(i)$ is the price of $X_t(i)$ for $i \in [1, N]$. Differentiating (12.5) with respect to L_t and $X_t(i)$ yields

$$\frac{\partial \Pi_t}{\partial L_t} = (1 - \alpha) L_t^{-\alpha} \sum_{i=1}^{N} X_t^{\alpha}(i) - W_t = (1 - \alpha) \frac{Y_t}{L_t} - W_t = 0, \quad (12.6)$$

$$\frac{\partial \Pi_t}{\partial X_t(i)} = \alpha L_t^{1-\alpha} X_t^{\alpha-1}(i) - P_t(i) = 0. \qquad (12.7)$$

These two sets of equations are the demand functions for L_t and $X_t(i)$ for $i \in [1, N]$.

12.3.   Intermediate Goods

Each variety of intermediate goods is produced by a firm that has monopolistic power over this variety. We refer to each variety of intermediate goods as an industry, and let's consider an arbitrary industry i. In industry i, the monopolistic firm rents capital from the household to produce intermediate good i. We consider a simple production function given by

$$X_t(i) = K_t(i). \qquad (12.8)$$

In other words, one unit of capital produces one unit of intermediate good i. The profit function for intermediate-good firm i is

$$\pi_t(i) = P_t(i) X_t(i) - R_t K_t(i). \qquad (12.9)$$

Given that this firm acts as a monopolist, it chooses its price to maximise profit (rather than taking the price as given). Substituting (12.7) and (12.8) into (12.9) yields

$$\pi_t(i) = \alpha L_t^{1-\alpha} X_t^{\alpha}(i) - R_t X_t(i). \tag{12.10}$$

Differentiating $\pi_t(i)$ with respect to $X_t(i)$ yields

$$\frac{\partial \pi_t(i)}{\partial X_t(i)} = \alpha \underbrace{\alpha L_t^{1-\alpha} X_t^{\alpha-1}(i)}_{=P_t(i)} - R_t = 0. \tag{12.11}$$

Using (12.7), we can re-express (12.11) as $P_t(i) = R_t/\alpha > R_t$, where $1/\alpha > 1$ is the markup ratio. Due to this markup pricing, the intermediate-good sector generates positive monopolistic profits. As a result of these monopolistic profits, the decentralised economy has a different allocation of resources compared with the centralised economy as we show below.

12.4.   Aggregation

Equation (12.11) shows that $X_t(i) = (\alpha^2/R_t)^{1/(1-\alpha)} L_t$ is the same across all $i \in [1, N]$. Using this information, we impose symmetry on (12.4) to obtain

$$Y_t = L_t^{1-\alpha} N X_t^{\alpha}(i). \tag{12.12}$$

Then, we substitute the resource constraint on capital given by $X_t(i) = K_t(i) = K_t/N$ into (12.12) to derive the aggregate production function:

$$Y_t = L_t^{1-\alpha} N \left(\frac{K_t}{N}\right)^{\alpha} = N^{1-\alpha} K_t^{\alpha} L_t^{1-\alpha} = A K_t^{\alpha} L_t^{1-\alpha}, \tag{12.13}$$

where we have relabelled $N^{1-\alpha}$ as A. This aggregate production function is the same as before. In this economy, it is the number of differentiated products that determines the level of technology; in other words, a higher level of technology is driven by a larger number of differentiated products.

Setting $L_t = 1$ in (12.7) yields

$$P_t(i) = \alpha X_t^{\alpha-1}(i). \tag{12.14}$$

From (12.11), we know that $P_t(i) = R_t/\alpha$. Substituting this equation and the resource constraint $X_t(i) = K_t/N$ into (12.14) yields the market demand curve for capital as follows:

$$R_t = \alpha^2 \left(\frac{K_t}{N}\right)^{\alpha-1} = \alpha^2 A K_t^{\alpha-1}, \tag{12.15}$$

where the second equality follows from $N^{1-\alpha} = A$. We impose steady state on the household's consumption path to derive the long-run capital supply curve as

$$\frac{\dot{C}_t}{C_t} = 0 \Leftrightarrow R_t = \rho + \delta; \tag{12.16}$$

see Figure 12.1. Finally, combining capital demand in (12.15) and capital supply in (12.16) yields the steady-state equilibrium level of capital under monopolistic competition as

$$K_m^* = \left(\frac{\alpha^2 A}{\rho + \delta}\right)^{1/(1-\alpha)}, \tag{12.17}$$

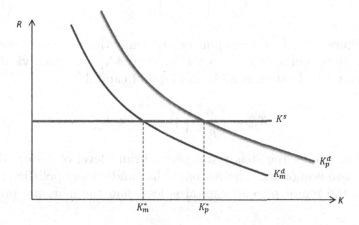

Figure 12.1. Monopolistic competition vs. perfect competition.

which is increasing in the level of technology A and decreasing in the discount rate ρ and the depreciation rate δ.

12.5. Monopolistic Competition vs. Perfect Competition

It may seem that the Ramsey model with a monopolistically competitive market in this chapter is very different from the Ramsey model with a perfectly competitive market in the previous chapter. However, the two models have the same aggregate structure: the same aggregate production function; the same capital-accumulation equation;[1] and the same consumption path (except that the equilibrium rental price of capital differs across the two models). We will use MPK_t to denote the marginal product of capital.

Regardless of the underlying market structure, the consumption path in the Ramsey model is

$$\frac{\dot{C}_t}{C_t} = R_t - \delta - \rho. \tag{12.18}$$

In a perfectly competitive market, the capital demand curve is $R_t = MPK_t = \alpha A K_t^{\alpha-1}$, which yields the following steady-state equilibrium level of capital:

$$K_p^* = \left(\frac{\alpha A}{\rho + \delta} \right)^{1/(1-\alpha)}; \tag{12.19}$$

see Figure 12.1. In a monopolistically competitive market, the capital demand curve is $R_t = \alpha MPK_t = \alpha^2 A K_t^{\alpha-1}$, which yields the following steady-state equilibrium level of capital:

$$K_m^* = \left(\frac{\alpha^2 A}{\rho + \delta} \right)^{1/(1-\alpha)} < K_p^*. \tag{12.20}$$

In other words, the steady-state equilibrium level of capital differs in the two economies. The reason is that under monopolistic competition, the rental price of capital is less than the marginal product

---

[1]One can show that $\dot{K}_t = R_t K_t + W_t + N\pi_t - C_t - \delta K_t = Y_t - C_t - \delta K_t$.

of capital (i.e., $R_t = \alpha MPK_t < MPK_t$ given $\alpha < 1$). Intuitively, due to monopolistic distortion, the market return to capital is lower under monopolistic competition than under perfect competition; as a result, the household accumulates less capital.

Finally, we derive the steady-state saving rate given by

$$s^* \equiv \frac{I^*}{Y^*} = \frac{\delta K^*}{A(K^*)^\alpha} = \frac{\delta(K^*)^{1-\alpha}}{A}. \tag{12.21}$$

In the Ramsey model with a monopolistically competitive market, the household's saving rate s_m^* is given by

$$s_m^* = \frac{\alpha^2 \delta}{\rho + \delta} < \frac{\alpha \delta}{\rho + \delta} = s_p^*. \tag{12.22}$$

Given an empirically relevant range of capital intensity $\alpha \in [1/3, 1/2]$, the distortion of monopolistic competition can cause the household's saving rate to be less than half of the optimal level. This distortion on the saving rate in turn reduces the level of output significantly; to see this,

$$\frac{Y_m^*}{Y_p^*} = \frac{A(K_m^*)^\alpha}{A(K_p^*)^\alpha} = \alpha^{\alpha/(1-\alpha)}. \tag{12.23}$$

For example, if $\alpha = 1/2$, then the monopolistic level of output Y_m^* is only half of the competitive level of output Y_p^*.

12.6. Market Power of Monopolistic Firms

Suppose the government imposes an upper bound on the monopolistic price given by

$$P_t(i) = \mu R_t < R_t/\alpha, \tag{12.24}$$

where the policy parameter $\mu \in (1, 1/\alpha)$ determines the markup ratio, capturing the market power of monopolistic firms. Substituting (12.24) and the resource constraint $X_t(i) = K_t/N$ into (12.14) yields

$$R_t = \frac{\alpha}{\mu}\left(\frac{K_t}{N}\right)^{\alpha-1} = \frac{\alpha A K_t^{\alpha-1}}{\mu} = \frac{MPK_t}{\mu}, \tag{12.25}$$

where the second equality follows from $N^{1-\alpha} = A$. Equation (12.25) shows that the difference between the marginal product of capital and its rental price is increasing in μ, which in turn determines the degree of distortion in the market economy.

Substituting the consumption path in (12.16) into (12.25) yields the steady-state equilibrium level of capital given by

$$K_m^* = \left[\frac{\alpha A}{\mu(\rho + \delta)} \right]^{1/(1-\alpha)} < \left(\frac{\alpha A}{\rho + \delta} \right)^{1/(1-\alpha)}, \qquad (12.26)$$

unless $\mu \to 1$. Similarly, the household's saving rate is given by

$$s_m^* \equiv \frac{I^*}{Y^*} = \frac{\delta K^*}{A(K^*)^\alpha} = \frac{\delta(K^*)^{1-\alpha}}{A} = \frac{\alpha\delta}{\mu(\rho + \delta)} < \frac{\alpha\delta}{\rho + \delta}, \qquad (12.27)$$

unless $\mu \to 1$. In other words, as μ approaches unity, K_m^* and s_m^* under monopolistic competition coincide with their equilibrium levels under perfect competition. Therefore, the market equilibrium allocations in the decentralised Ramsey model with monopolistic competition can be socially optimal if the government completely removes the market power of monopolistic firms by restricting the markup ratio μ to unity.

12.7. Summary

In this chapter, we introduce an alternative market structure into the Ramsey model. Specifically, we consider a monopolistically competitive product market. In this case, each of the monopolistic firms sells a differentiated product. As a result, the monopolistic firms have market power and charge a markup over their marginal cost of production. This monopolistic distortion causes the rental price to be less than the marginal product of capital. As a result, the household accumulates less capital and chooses a lower saving rate than the socially optimal level. In other words, due to the presence of monopolistic distortion in the economy, the market equilibrium is inefficient. Therefore, the first fundamental theorem of welfare economics does not hold in the Ramsey model with a monopolistically competitive product market unless the government removes the monopolistic distortion in the economy.

12.8.   Exercises

1. Suppose the policy parameter $\mu \in (1, 1/\alpha)$ determines the markup ratio. Compare the steady-state saving rate from the monopolistic version of the Ramsey model to the consumption-maximising saving rate s in the Solow model. Which one is higher? Under what conditions would they be the same?

2. Suppose $L_t = L$. Derive the steady-state saving rate in the monopolistic version of the Ramsey model.

3. Consider the introduction of leisure to the household's utility function:

$$U = \int_0^\infty e^{-\rho t}[\ln C_t + \beta \ln(1 - l_t)]dt, \qquad (12.28)$$

where the parameter $\beta > 0$ determines the importance of leisure $1 - l_t$ in the utility function. In this case, the asset-accumulation equation becomes

$$\dot{K}_t = R_t K_t + W_t l_t + \sum_{i=1}^{N} \pi_t(i) - C_t - \delta K_t. \qquad (12.29)$$

Suppose we assume $\mu \in (1, 1/\alpha)$. Show that the steady-state equilibrium level of labour l^* is given by

$$l^* = \frac{1}{1 + \frac{\beta}{1-\alpha}\left[1 - \frac{\alpha\delta}{\mu(\rho+\delta)}\right]}, \qquad (12.30)$$

which is less than l^* in (11.19) in the competitive market of the Ramsey model unless $\delta = 0$.[2]

4. Suppose the growth rate of labour is $\dot{L}_t/L_t = n$. Derive the steady-state saving rate in the monopolistic version of the Ramsey model.

---

[2]Although there is no distortion in the labour market (i.e., $W_t = (1 - \alpha)Y_t/l_t$), the monopolistic distortion in the capital market leads to a suboptimally low investment rate s^* and a suboptimally high consumption rate $C^*/Y^* = 1 - s^*$, which in turn leads to a suboptimally high level of leisure $1 - l^*$ unless $s^* = \delta = 0$.

Chapter 13

The Romer Model of Endogenous Technological Change

Paul Romer greatly enhances economists' understanding of endogenous technological change by developing a growth model in which technological progress is driven by the invention of new products, which in turn is due to research and development (R&D) by profit-seeking entrepreneurs. In this chapter, we cover the Romer model.[1] In the previous chapter, we introduced a monopolistically competitive market structure to the Ramsey model. If we further introduce an R&D sector into the model to allow for endogenous growth in the number of products, then we have the Romer model. In other words, we have added several layers of structure to gradually extend the familiar Solow model into the less familiar Romer model.[2] Once we derive the endogenous growth rate of technology in the Romer model, we can then perform comparative statics to explore the determinants of technological progress.

As before, there is a representative firm that produces the final good, and there are a number of firms that produce differentiated intermediate goods. The novel element here is that the number of these differentiated goods increases over time due to innovation. Because each of these intermediate-good firms sells a differentiated

---

[1]The Romer model was developed by Romer (1990), who received the Nobel Memorial Prize in Economics in 2018 partly for this contribution.

[2]See Chu (2018) for this approach of teaching the Romer model. Some discussion in this chapter follows from Chu (2018).

product, it generates monopolistic profits, which serve as the incentives for R&D. In summary, the model has the following components: (a) a representative household, (b) a representative firm that produces the final good, (c) a number of monopolistic firms that produce differentiated intermediate goods, and (d) competitive R&D entrepreneurs who invest in R&D and create new varieties of intermediate goods.

13.1. Household

The representative household has the following lifetime utility function:

$$U = \int_0^\infty e^{-\rho t} \ln C_t dt,$$

where the parameter $\rho > 0$ is the household's discount rate and C_t is the level of consumption at time t. The household inelastically supplies L units[3] of labour to earn a wage income W_t. Furthermore, it accumulates capital K_t and rents it to firms to earn a capital-rental income R_t. Here, we also introduce financial asset F_t (i.e., the shares of monopolistic firms) and its rate of return given by r_t, which is also the real interest rate. Then, the asset-accumulation equation becomes[4]

$$\dot{F}_t + \dot{K}_t = r_t F_t + R_t K_t + W_t L - C_t - \delta K_t,$$

where the parameter $\delta > 0$ is the depreciation rate of capital.

The Hamiltonian function is given by

$$H_t = \ln C_t + \lambda_t (r_t F_t + R_t K_t + W_t L - C_t - \delta K_t).$$

The first-order conditions include

$$\frac{\partial H_t}{\partial C_t} = \frac{1}{C_t} - \lambda_t = 0,$$

---

[3]Here, we consider L units of labour supply instead of 1 unit for reasons to be explained.

[4]It can be shown that the asset-accumulation equation can be re-expressed as $\dot{K}_t = Y_t - C_t - \delta K_t$ in equilibrium.

$$\frac{\partial H_t}{\partial K_t} = \lambda_t(R_t - \delta) = \lambda_t\rho - \dot{\lambda}_t, \tag{13.1}$$

$$\frac{\partial H_t}{\partial F_t} = \lambda_t r_t = \lambda_t\rho - \dot{\lambda}_t, \tag{13.2}$$

where F_t is also a state variable. Combining (13.1) and (13.2) yields a no-arbitrage condition given by $r_t = R_t - \delta$. In other words, the two types of assets (F_t and K_t) must yield the same rate of return. We have the consumption path given by

$$\frac{\dot{C}_t}{C_t} = r_t - \rho, \tag{13.3}$$

where $r_t = R_t - \delta$ from the no-arbitrage condition. Usually, the consumption path is expressed in r_t instead of $R_t - \delta$.

13.2.   Final Good

There is a representative firm that produces the final good Y_t. This firm hires labour and uses intermediate goods $X_t(i)$ as inputs. The production function is almost the same as in Chapter 12 and given by

$$Y_t = L_{Y,t}^{1-\alpha} \int_0^{N_t} X_t^\alpha(i)di, \tag{13.4}$$

where the parameter $\alpha \in (0,1)$ determines the intensity $1 - \alpha$ of production labour. $L_{Y,t}$ is the number of production workers (and we will use $L_{R,t}$ to denote R&D workers such that the resource constraint on labour is given by $L_{Y,t} + L_{R,t} = L$). It is useful to note that we are treating the number of varieties N_t as a continuous number (instead of a discrete number) for modelling simplicity. The profit function for the final-good firm is

$$\Pi_t = Y_t - W_t L_{Y,t} - \int_0^{N_t} P_t(i)X_t(i)di, \tag{13.5}$$

where we have implicitly chosen Y_t as the numeraire and $P_t(i)$ is the price of $X_t(i)$ for $i \in [1, N]$. Differentiating (13.5) with respect to

$L_{Y,t}$ and $X_t(i)$ yields

$$\frac{\partial \Pi_t}{\partial L_{Y,t}} = (1-\alpha)L_{Y,t}^{-\alpha} \int_0^{N_t} X_t^{\alpha}(i)di - W_t$$

$$= (1-\alpha)\frac{Y_t}{L_{Y,t}} - W_t = 0, \qquad (13.6)$$

$$\frac{\partial \Pi_t}{\partial X_t(i)} = \alpha L_{Y,t}^{1-\alpha} X_t^{\alpha-1}(i) - P_t(i) = 0, \qquad (13.7)$$

for $i \in [0, N_t]$. These two sets of equations are the demand functions for $L_{Y,t}$ and $X_t(i)$ for $i \in [0, N_t]$.

13.3. Intermediate Goods

This sector is exactly the same as in Chapter 12. Each variety of intermediate goods is produced by a firm that has monopolistic power over this variety. We will refer to each variety of intermediate goods as an industry, and let's consider an arbitrary industry i. In industry i, the monopolistic firm rents capital from the household to produce the intermediate good. We consider a simple production function as before.

$$X_t(i) = K_t(i). \qquad (13.8)$$

In other words, one unit of capital produces one unit of intermediate good. The profit function for this intermediate-good firm is

$$\pi_t(i) = P_t(i)X_t(i) - R_t K_t(i). \qquad (13.9)$$

Given that this firm acts as a monopolist, it chooses its price to maximise profit (rather than taking the price as given). Substituting (13.7) and (13.8) into (13.9) yields

$$\pi_t(i) = \alpha L_{Y,t}^{1-\alpha} X_t^{\alpha}(i) - R_t X_t(i). \qquad (13.10)$$

Differentiating $\pi_t(i)$ with respect to $X_t(i)$ yields

$$\frac{\partial \pi_t(i)}{\partial X_t(i)} = \alpha \underbrace{\alpha L_{Y,t}^{1-\alpha} X_t^{\alpha-1}(i)}_{=P_t(i)} - R_t = 0. \qquad (13.11)$$

Using (13.7), we can re-express (13.11) as $P_t(i) = R_t/\alpha > R_t$, where $1/\alpha > 1$ is the markup ratio. Due to this markup pricing, the intermediate-good sector generates positive monopolistic profits.

13.4. R&D

The novel element in the Romer model is the R&D sector. The law of motion for the number of varieties is given by

$$\dot{N}_t = \theta N_t L_{R,t}, \tag{13.12}$$

where $L_{R,t}$ is the number of R&D workers and $\theta > 0$ is an R&D productivity parameter. Rewriting (13.12) yields the growth rate of N_t given by $g_N \equiv \dot{N}_t/N_t = \theta L_{R,t}$; therefore, increasing R&D labour stimulates economic growth. However, what determines the equilibrium allocation of R&D labour $L_{R,t}$?

Let v_t denote the market value of a new invention (i.e., a new variety of differentiated products). The market value of creating $\dot{N}_t$ new inventions is $\dot{N}_t v_t$. The cost of R&D is $W_t L_{R,t}$. Given that there is free entry in the R&D sector, this sector generates zero profit such that

$$\dot{N}_t v_t = W_t L_{R,t}. \tag{13.13}$$

Substituting (13.12) into (13.13), we obtain

$$\theta N_t v_t = W_t, \tag{13.14}$$

where we have cancelled $L_{R,t}$ from both sides.

We will see that the R&D condition in (13.14) determines the equilibrium allocation of R&D labour. To show this result, we will need to find out the value of v_t. The value of an invention is the present value of all the future monopolistic profits. Formally,

$$v_t = \frac{\pi_t}{r - g_\pi}, \tag{13.15}$$

where g_π is the steady-state equilibrium growth rate of π_t. Substituting (13.15) into (13.14) yields

$$\frac{\theta N_t \pi_t}{r - g_\pi} = W_t. \tag{13.16}$$

We already know from (13.6) that $W_t = (1-\alpha)Y_t/L_{Y,t}$. We also know from (13.3) that $r = \rho + g_C$, where g_C is the steady-state equilibrium growth rate of C_t. Therefore, what we need to do next is to derive an expression for π_t.

13.5.   Aggregation

Equation (13.11) implies that $X_t(i) = (\alpha^2/R_t)^{1/(1-\alpha)}L_{Y,t}$ is the same across all $i \in [0, N_t]$. Using this information, we impose symmetry on (13.4) to obtain $Y_t = L_{Y,t}^{1-\alpha}N_t X_t^\alpha(i)$. Then, we substitute into this equation the resource constraint on capital given by $X_t(i) = K_t(i) = K_t/N_t$ to derive the aggregate production function:

$$Y_t = L_{Y,t}^{1-\alpha}N_t \left(\frac{K_t}{N_t}\right)^\alpha = N_t^{1-\alpha}K_t^\alpha L_{Y,t}^{1-\alpha} = A_t K_t^\alpha L_{Y,t}^{1-\alpha}, \qquad (13.17)$$

where we have relabelled $N_t^{1-\alpha}$ as A_t. Therefore, the growth rate of A_t in the Solow model becomes $g_A = (1-\alpha)g_N$, which is endogenous in the Romer model. Also, it should be noted that the aggregate production function is the same as the one in the Solow model except that L_t is replaced by $L_{Y,t}$.

Recall that the profit function for the intermediate-good firm i is

$$\pi_t(i) = P_t(i)X_t(i) - R_t K_t(i).$$

Substituting (13.8) and $P_t(i) = R_t/\alpha$ into the profit function yields

$$\pi_t = \frac{1-\alpha}{\alpha}R_t K_t(i) = \frac{1-\alpha}{\alpha}\frac{R_t K_t}{N_t}, \qquad (13.18)$$

which uses the resource constraint $X_t(i) = K_t(i) = K_t/N_t$. Recall from (13.6) that the production labour income share of output is $W_t L_{Y,t} = (1-\alpha)Y_t$, which implies that the remaining share of output αY_t goes to capital income and monopolistic profit[5]:

$$\pi_t N_t + R_t K_t = N_t P_t X_t = \alpha Y_t. \qquad (13.19)$$

---

[5]Note that GDP in this economy is given by $GDP_t = Y_t + R\&D_t = Y_t + W_t L_{R,t}$.

Combining (13.18) and (13.19) yields the profit share of output given by

$$\pi_t = \alpha(1-\alpha)\frac{Y_t}{N_t}, \tag{13.20}$$

which implies that $g_\pi = g_Y - g_N$.

13.6. Solving the Model

Using (13.20) along with $W_t = (1-\alpha)Y_t/L_{Y,t}$ and $r = \rho + g_C$, we can simplify (13.16) to

$$\frac{\alpha\theta}{\rho + g_C - g_Y + g_N} = \frac{1}{L_Y}. \tag{13.21}$$

On the balanced growth path, the growth rates of output and consumption are the same such that $g_C = g_Y$. Using $g_N = \theta L_R$ from (13.12), we can further simplify (13.21) to

$$\frac{\alpha\theta}{\rho + \theta L_R} = \frac{1}{L_Y}. \tag{13.22}$$

Combining (13.22) with the resource constraint on labour $L_Y + L_R = L$ yields

$$L_R = \frac{\alpha}{1+\alpha}\left(L - \frac{\rho}{\alpha\theta}\right). \tag{13.23}$$

Therefore, the equilibrium allocation of R&D labour has the following comparative statics:

$$L_R(\underset{-}{\rho}, \underset{+}{\theta}, \underset{+}{\alpha}, \underset{+}{L}).$$

The intuition of these comparative statics results can be explained as follows.

13.6.1. *R&D productivity*

An improvement in R&D productivity θ increases the growth rate g_N of technology for a given level of R&D labour L_R and also makes R&D labour more productive, which in turn increases R&D labour in the economy. Therefore, g_N is increasing in θ. To see this, recall that the growth rate of technology is $g_N = \theta L_R(\theta)$. Therefore, an increase in R&D productivity θ has a direct positive effect on g_N by increasing R&D productivity and also an indirect positive effect by increasing R&D labour L_R. The parameter θ captures the importance of human capital on the innovation capacity of an economy. To stimulate economic growth, policymakers could consider devoting more resources to education that improves the innovative capacity of entrepreneurs, scientists and engineers.

13.6.2. *Discount rate*

A higher discount rate ρ increases the real interest rate and decreases the present value of monopolistic profits as well as the value of inventions, which in turn decreases R&D labour in the economy. Therefore, g_N is decreasing in ρ. To see this, recall that the growth rate of technology is $g_N = \theta L_R(\rho)$. Therefore, an increase in the discount rate ρ decreases the growth rate of technology by decreasing R&D labour L_R. The parameter ρ captures the effects of household preference and also frictions in the financial market, such as credit constraints, on innovation. To stimulate economic growth, policymakers could consider policies that improve the efficiency of the financial market.

13.6.3. *Capital and labour intensity in production*

An increase in α increases capital intensity and reduces labour intensity in the production process, allowing more labour to be devoted to R&D. Therefore, g_N is increasing in α. To see this, recall that the growth rate of the number of differentiated products is $g_N = \theta L_R(\alpha)$. Therefore, an increase in capital intensity α increases the growth rate of technology by increasing R&D labour L_R. The parameter α captures the effect of structural transformation of an economy from a labour-intensive production process to a capital-intensive production process. However, the positive effect of α on R&D is based on the assumption that R&D does not require the use of capital. If R&D also uses capital, then the effect of α on growth may be reversed depending on the degree of capital intensity in the R&D process.

13.6.4. *Labour force*

Finally, a larger labour force L increases the supply of labour in the economy, which in turn increases R&D labour and the growth rate of technology. Therefore, g_N is increasing in L. To see this, recall that the growth rate of technology is $g_N = \theta L_R(L)$. Therefore, an increase in the labour force L increases the growth rate of technology by increasing R&D labour L_R. In the literature, this is known as the scale effect, which is often viewed as a counterfactual implication of the Romer model. We will discuss the scale effect in more detail in Chapter 14.

13.7.   Summary

In this chapter, we develop the Romer model by introducing an R&D sector into the Ramsey model with a monopolistically competitive product market. In this case, the positive monopolistic profit in the economy serves as an incentive for entrepreneurs to do R&D, which in turn gives rise to technological progress. We derive the market equilibrium level of R&D labour, which determines the equilibrium growth rate of technology. In summary, the market equilibrium level of R&D labour is increasing in the monopolistic power of firms (see Exercise 1), the productivity of R&D, the degree of capital intensity in production and the size of the labour force but decreasing in the discount rate of the representative household. Therefore, cross-country variation in these determinants helps to explain some of the variation in economic growth across countries.

13.8.   Exercises

1. Suppose the government imposes an upper bound on the monopolistic price given by

$$P_t(i) = \mu R_t < R_t/\alpha, \qquad (13.24)$$

where the parameter $\mu \in (1, 1/\alpha)$ is the markup ratio, capturing the monopolistic power of firms. Show that the equilibrium allocation of R&D labour becomes

$$L_R = \alpha \left[\frac{\mu - 1}{\mu - \alpha} L - \frac{\mu(1 - \alpha)}{\mu - \alpha} \frac{\rho}{\alpha\theta} \right], \qquad (13.25)$$

which is increasing in the monopolistic power μ of firms.

2. Show that on the balanced growth path, the growth rate of capital, output and consumption is given by g_N.

3. Show that on the balanced growth path, the saving rate s^* in the Romer model is given by

$$s^* = \frac{\alpha}{\mu} \frac{\delta + g_N}{\rho + \delta + g_N}. \tag{13.26}$$

4. Suppose the production function in the Romer model is given by

$$Y_t = H_{Y,t}^{1-\alpha-\beta} L_t^{\beta} \int_0^{N_t} X_t^{\alpha}(i)\, di,$$

where $H_{Y,t}$ is the number of high-skill production workers, and L_t is the number of low-skill workers. The law of motion for the number of varieties is given by

$$\dot{N}_t = \theta N_t H_{R,t},$$

where $H_{R,t}$ is the number of high-skill R&D workers. The household inelastically supplies L units of low-skill labour to earn a low-skill wage income W_t, and inelastically supplies H units of high-skill labour to earn a high-skill wage income ω_t. In this case, the asset-accumulation equation becomes

$$\dot{F}_t + \dot{K}_t = r_t F_t + R_t K_t + W_t L + \omega_t H - C_t - \delta K_t.$$

Derive the equilibrium allocation of high-skill R&D labour H_R and the growth rate of output on the BGP.

Chapter 14

Scale Effect in the Romer Model

In this chapter, we will explore an important but counterfactual property of the Romer model. Recall from the Romer model the following key equation:

$$g_N \equiv \dot{N}_t/N_t = \theta L_{R,t},$$

where $L_{R,t}$ is the number of R&D workers and $\theta > 0$ is an R&D productivity parameter. This equation implies that the growth rate g_N of technology is increasing in the number of R&D workers $L_{R,t}$. This property is known as the scale effect in the literature. Jones (1995) points out that this prediction from the Romer model is inconsistent with empirical evidence. Jones (1995) documents that the number of R&D scientists in the US steadily increased from 1950 to the late 1980s; however, the growth rate of technology did not exhibit any positive trend during this period; see Figures 14.1 and 14.2 in which we look at more recent data from 1990 to 2013.[1] Motivated by this empirical fact, Jones developed a modified version of the Romer model, which is free from the scale effect.

---

[1]The trend of total factor productivity (TFP) growth rates is computed using the HP filter.

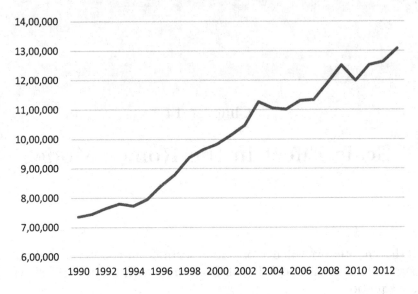

Figure 14.1.   Researchers in the US.

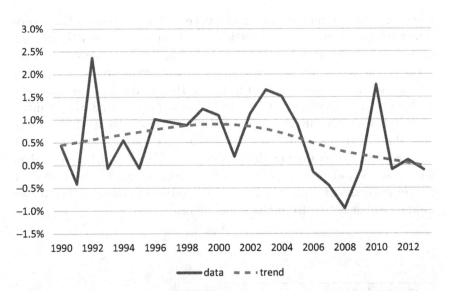

Figure 14.2.   TFP growth in the US.

14.1. The Jones Model

The basic structure of the Jones model is the same as the Romer model. The only major difference is in the law of motion for the number of varieties. Romer (1990) assumes the following law of motion:

$$\dot{N}_t = \theta N_t L_{R,t}. \tag{14.1}$$

Jones (1995) generalises this specification to

$$\dot{N}_t = \theta N_t^{\phi} L_{R,t}, \tag{14.2}$$

where the parameter $\phi < 1$ measures the degree of intertemporal knowledge spillovers. In other words, Romer (1990) implicitly assumes that $\phi = 1$. In contrast, Jones (1995) relaxes this assumption and considers the general case of $\phi < 1$. To see the different implications, we divide (14.2) by N_t to obtain

$$\frac{\dot{N}_t}{N_t} = \theta \frac{L_{R,t}}{N_t^{1-\phi}}. \tag{14.3}$$

On the balanced growth path, the growth rate $\dot{N}_t/N_t$ is constant, which in turn implies that $L_{R,t}$ and $N_t^{1-\phi}$ grow at the same rate; formally,

$$(1-\phi)\frac{\dot{N}_t}{N_t} = \frac{\dot{L}_{R,t}}{L_{R,t}} \Leftrightarrow \frac{\dot{N}_t}{N_t} = \frac{1}{1-\phi}\frac{\dot{L}_{R,t}}{L_{R,t}}. \tag{14.4}$$

Therefore, the long-run growth rate of technology is now determined by the *growth rate* of $L_{R,t}$ instead of the *level* of $L_{R,t}$, eliminating the scale effect. Figure 14.3 presents the growth rate of researchers and shows that its trend exhibits a similar pattern as the trend of TFP growth rates in Figure 14.2.

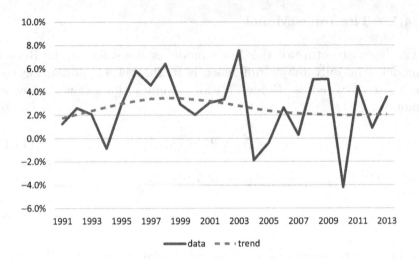

Figure 14.3.   Growth of US researchers.

14.2.   Solving the Model

As mentioned before, the basic structure of the Jones model is the same as in the Romer model, so we do not repeat all the equations here. The key difference is in Equation (14.2). Furthermore, the Jones model allows for growth in the labour force L_t, which increases over time at a constant exogenous growth rate n. On the balanced growth path, the resource constraint on labour given by

$$L_{R,t} + L_{Y,t} = L_t \Leftrightarrow \frac{L_{R,t}}{L_t} + \frac{L_{Y,t}}{L_t} = 1 \qquad (14.5)$$

implies that $L_{R,t}/L_t$ must be constant. Therefore, $L_{R,t}$ and L_t grow at the same rate on the balanced growth path. Using this information along with (14.4), we find that the steady-state equilibrium growth rate of N_t is

$$g_N = \frac{n}{1 - \phi}, \qquad (14.6)$$

which is determined by exogenous parameters n and ϕ. Therefore, the Jones model is also known as the semi-endogenous growth model.[2]

---

[2]See Cozzi (2017a, b) for a hybrid growth model that captures both semi-endogenous growth and fully endogenous growth.

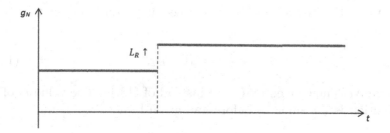

Figure 14.4.   Romer model.

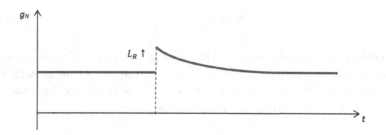

Figure 14.5.   Jones model.

Increasing R&D labour $L_{R,t}$ only leads to a higher growth rate in the short run. From the following equation, we see that for a given N_t, an increase in R&D labour $L_{R,t}$ raises the growth rate $\dot{N}_t/N_t$ temporarily.

$$\frac{\dot{N}_t}{N_t} = \theta \frac{L_{R,t}}{N_t^{1-\phi}}.$$

However, $N_t^{1-\phi}$ increases over time to offset the effect of $L_{R,t}$. Eventually, the growth rate $\dot{N}_t/N_t$ returns to $g_N = n/(1 - \phi)$ in the long run; see Figures 14.4 and 14.5 for a comparison between the Romer model and the Jones model.

The steady-state equilibrium growth rate g_N is easy to determine in the Jones model. However, we will have to go through the same derivations as in the Romer model to derive the steady-state equilibrium allocation of R&D labour, which determines the growth rate of technology in the short run and the level of technology in the long run.

As in the Romer model, the free-entry condition in the R&D sector is

$$\dot{N}_t v_t = W_t L_{R,t},\tag{14.7}$$

where $\dot{N}_t$ is now given by (14.2) instead of (14.1). The value v_t of an invention is the same as before and given by

$$v_t = \frac{\pi_t}{r - g_\pi},\tag{14.8}$$

where monopolistic profit π_t is also the same as before and given by

$$\pi_t = \alpha(1 - \alpha)\frac{Y_t}{N_t}.\tag{14.9}$$

Therefore, the steady-state equilibrium growth rate of π_t is the same as before and given by $g_\pi = g_Y - g_N$, where g_Y is the growth rate of output Y_t. Similarly, the wage rate W_t is equal to the marginal product of production labour $L_{Y,t}$ as before and given by

$$W_t = (1 - \alpha)\frac{Y_t}{L_{Y,t}}.\tag{14.10}$$

Substituting (14.8), (14.9) and (14.10) into (14.7) yields

$$\frac{\alpha}{r - g_\pi}\frac{\dot{N}_t}{N_t} = \frac{L_{R,t}}{L_{Y,t}},\tag{14.11}$$

where $\dot{N}_t/N_t = g_N = n/(1 - \phi)$. Combining the real interest rate r from the consumption path $r = \rho + g_C$ with $g_\pi = g_Y - g_N$ yields

$$r - g_\pi = \rho + g_N = \rho + n/(1 - \phi),\tag{14.12}$$

where we have used the steady-state condition $g_C = g_Y$, equating the growth rate of consumption to the growth rate of output. Finally, if we define $S_R \equiv L_R/L_Y$ as the steady-state equilibrium ratio of R&D labour L_R to production labour L_Y, then Equation (14.11) becomes

$$S_R = \frac{\alpha g_N}{\rho + g_N} = \frac{\alpha n/(1 - \phi)}{\rho + n/(1 - \phi)} = \frac{\alpha n}{(1 - \phi)\rho + n}.\tag{14.13}$$

Therefore, the steady-state equilibrium ratio of R&D labour to production labour has the following comparative statics:

$$S_R(\underset{-}{\rho}, \underset{+}{\phi}, \underset{+}{\alpha}, \underset{+}{n}).$$

Intuitively, a higher discount rate ρ increases the real interest rate and decreases the present value of monopolistic profits. A larger α increases capital intensity and reduces labour intensity in the production process, allowing more labour to be devoted to R&D. An increase in either knowledge spillover ϕ or population growth n raises the technology growth rate g_N, which in turn increases the benefit of R&D.

14.3. Summary

In this chapter, we explore the scale effect in the Romer model, in which the steady-state growth rate of technology is increasing in the level of R&D labour. This implication is inconsistent with the evidence documented in Jones (1995), who then generalises the Romer model by parameterising the degree of intertemporal knowledge spillovers and restricting this parameter value to be less than unity. In this case, the steady-state growth rate of technology depends on the growth rate of R&D labour (instead of its level), removing the scale effect in the Romer model. Then, we derive the market equilibrium allocation of R&D labour and explore its determinants. In this case, we find that the growth rate of the labour force and the degree of intertemporal knowledge spillovers also affect the market equilibrium allocation of R&D labour.

14.4. Exercises

1. Suppose the government imposes an upper bound on the monopolistic price given by

$$P_t(i) = \mu R_t < R_t/\alpha, \tag{14.14}$$

where the parameter $\mu \in (1, 1/\alpha)$ is the markup ratio, capturing the monopolistic power of firms. Show that the equilibrium ratio of R&D labour to production labour becomes

$$S_R = \frac{\mu - 1}{\mu(1 - \alpha)} \frac{\alpha g_N}{\rho + g_N} = \frac{\mu - 1}{\mu(1 - \alpha)} \frac{\alpha n}{(1 - \phi)\rho + n}, \quad (14.15)$$

which is increasing in the monopolistic power μ of firms.

2. Show that on the balanced growth path, the growth rate of capital, output and consumption is given by $g_N + n$.

3. Show that on the balanced growth path, the saving rate s^* in the Jones model is given by

$$s^* = \frac{\alpha}{\mu} \frac{\delta + g_N + n}{\rho + \delta + g_N + n}. \quad (14.16)$$

4. Consider the introduction of leisure to the household's utility function in the Jones model:

$$U = \int_0^\infty e^{-\rho t} \left[\ln C_t + \beta \ln (1 - l_t) \right] dt,$$

where the parameter $\beta > 0$ determines the importance of leisure $1 - l_t$ in the utility function. In this case, the asset-accumulation equation becomes

$$\dot{F}_t + \dot{K}_t = r_t F_t + R_t K_t + W_t l_t - C_t - \delta K_t.$$

Suppose we assume $\mu \in (1, 1/\alpha)$. Derive the equilibrium allocation of R&D labour L_R and the growth rate of output on the BGP.

Chapter 15

R&D Underinvestment
and Subsidies

In this chapter, we will compare the decentralised equilibrium allocation in the Jones model to its socially optimal allocation chosen by a social planner. As we will show, due to the presence of R&D externality, the market equilibrium level of R&D labour is lower than its socially optimal level. In other words, as a result of market failure, the market economy exhibits a social problem of R&D underinvestment. In this case, it is socially optimal for the government to provide policy intervention in the form of R&D subsidy.

Recall that the law of motion for the number of varieties in the Jones model is given by

$$\dot{N}_t = \theta N_t^\phi L_{R,t},$$

where $L_{R,t}$ is the number of R&D workers and $\theta > 0$ is an R&D productivity parameter. For simplicity, we will consider a special case of $\phi = 0$ (i.e., zero knowledge spillovers), so that the law of motion for the number of varieties simplifies to $\dot{N}_t = \theta L_{R,t}$. In this case, the steady-state equilibrium ratio of R&D labour to production labour in the Jones model simplifies to

$$S_R = \frac{\alpha g_N}{\rho + g_N} = \frac{\alpha n}{\rho + n}, \tag{15.1}$$

where we have set $\phi = 0$ and $g_N = n$.

15.1.   Socially Optimal Level of R&D

To derive the socially optimal allocation in the Jones model, we first write down its key equations. The representative household has the following lifetime utility function:

$$U = \int_0^\infty e^{-\rho t} \ln C_t dt, \tag{15.2}$$

where the parameter $\rho > 0$ is the household's discount rate and C_t is the level of consumption at time t. The aggregate production function for output Y_t is given by

$$Y_t = N_t^{1-\alpha} K_t^\alpha L_{Y,t}^{1-\alpha}, \tag{15.3}$$

where the parameter $\alpha \in (0,1)$ determines the intensity $1 - \alpha$ of production labour $L_{Y,t}$. The accumulation equation of capital K_t is

$$\dot{K}_t = Y_t - C_t - \delta K_t, \tag{15.4}$$

where the parameter $\delta > 0$ is the depreciation rate of capital. The law of motion for the number of varieties is

$$\dot{N}_t = \theta L_{R,t}. \tag{15.5}$$

Finally, the resource constraint on labour is

$$L_{R,t} + L_{Y,t} = L_t, \tag{15.6}$$

where the labour force L_t grows at a constant exogenous growth rate n. Given that we are deriving the socially optimal allocation, we are solving the centralised version of the model. In other words, we are not dealing with the market equilibrium, but instead, we directly maximise the household's utility in (15.2) subject to (15.3)–(15.6).

For convenience, we will drop all the time subscripts. The Hamiltonian function is

$$H = \ln C + \lambda_K (N^{1-\alpha} K^\alpha L_Y^{1-\alpha} - C - \delta K_t) + \lambda_N \theta (L - L_Y), \tag{15.7}$$

where λ_K is the multiplier for $\dot{K}$ and λ_N is the multiplier for $\dot{N}$. The first-order conditions are

$$\frac{\partial H}{\partial C} = \frac{1}{C} - \lambda_K = 0, \tag{15.8}$$

$$\frac{\partial H}{\partial L_Y} = \lambda_K(1-\alpha)\frac{Y}{L_Y} - \lambda_N\theta = 0, \tag{15.9}$$

$$\frac{\partial H}{\partial K} = \lambda_K\left(\alpha\frac{Y}{K} - \delta\right) = \lambda_K\rho - \dot{\lambda}_K, \tag{15.10}$$

$$\frac{\partial H}{\partial N} = \lambda_K(1-\alpha)\frac{Y}{N} = \lambda_N\rho - \dot{\lambda}_N. \tag{15.11}$$

Equation (15.9) can be re-expressed as

$$\frac{(1-\alpha)\lambda_K Y}{\lambda_N} = \theta L_Y. \tag{15.12}$$

On the balanced growth path (BGP), the growth rate of Y and C is[1]

$$g_Y = g_C = g_N + n = 2n, \tag{15.13}$$

where the second equality holds due to $\phi = 0$ and $g_N = n$. Rewriting (15.11) yields

$$\frac{(1-\alpha)\lambda_K Y}{\lambda_N N} = \rho - \frac{\dot{\lambda}_N}{\lambda_N}, \tag{15.14}$$

where both sides are stationary in the long run. From (15.8), we have $\lambda_K C = 1$, which is stationary and implies that $\lambda_K Y$ is also stationary. Therefore, $\lambda_N N$ must be stationary, implying that $\dot{\lambda}_N/\lambda_N = -g_N = -n$. Now we can substitute (15.12) into (15.14) to obtain

$$\frac{\theta L_Y}{N} = \rho + n, \tag{15.15}$$

---

[1]One can use the production function in (15.3) and the long-run implication that the growth rate of output and capital is the same to derive this growth rate.

which also uses $-\dot{\lambda}_N/\lambda_N = n$. We use the law of motion for $\dot{N}$ to derive

$$\frac{\dot{N}}{N} = \theta\frac{L_R}{N} = n \Leftrightarrow N = \theta\frac{L_R}{n}. \tag{15.16}$$

Substituting (15.16) into (15.15) yields the socially optimal ratio S_R^* of R&D labour to production labour given by

$$S_R^* = \frac{n}{\rho + n}. \tag{15.17}$$

15.2.   R&D Underinvestment

Comparing (15.1) and (15.17) shows R&D underinvestment in the market economy:

$$S_R = \frac{\alpha n}{\rho + n} = \alpha S_R^*, \tag{15.18}$$

where $\alpha < 1$. For example, if $\alpha = 1/2$, then the market equilibrium R&D ratio S_R is only half of the optimal R&D ratio S_R^*. The decentralised equilibrium allocates too little labour to the R&D sector because the market economy does not provide enough incentives. To see this, it is useful to note that the marginal product of N_t is

$$\frac{\partial Y_t}{\partial N_t} = (1 - \alpha)\frac{Y_t}{N_t}, \tag{15.19}$$

but the market allocates less than this amount to monopolistic profit:

$$\pi_t = \alpha(1 - \alpha)\frac{Y_t}{N_t} = \alpha\frac{\partial Y_t}{\partial N_t}, \tag{15.20}$$

where $\alpha < 1$. Given that the social benefit of R&D (i.e., the marginal product of N_t) is larger than the private benefit to entrepreneurs (i.e., the monopolistic profit), this is a positive R&D externality, which is known as the surplus appropriability problem. To solve this R&D underinvestment problem, the government could make use of R&D subsidies, which we will analyse in the following section.

15.3. R&D Subsidies

We now determine the equilibrium allocation of R&D labour in the Jones model with R&D subsidies. We continue to focus on the special case with $\phi = 0$. The cost of R&D is $(1 - \varsigma)W_t L_{R,t}$, where $\varsigma \in [0, 1]$ is the rate of R&D subsidies provided by the government. Therefore, the zero-profit condition in the R&D sector is modified to

$$\dot{N}_t v_t = (1 - \varsigma)W_t L_{R,t}. \tag{15.21}$$

The value v_t of an invention is

$$v_t = \frac{\pi_t}{r - g_\pi}, \tag{15.22}$$

where the amount of monopolistic profit π_t is

$$\pi_t = \alpha(1 - \alpha)\frac{Y_t}{N_t}. \tag{15.23}$$

Therefore, the steady-state equilibrium growth rate of π_t is $g_\pi = g_Y - g_N$. The wage rate is

$$W_t = (1 - \alpha)\frac{Y_t}{L_{Y,t}}. \tag{15.24}$$

Substituting (15.22)–(15.24) into (15.21) yields

$$\frac{\alpha}{r - g_\pi}\frac{\dot{N}_t}{N_t} = (1 - \varsigma)\frac{L_{R,t}}{L_{Y,t}}, \tag{15.25}$$

where $\dot{N}_t/N_t = g_N = n$ (due to $\phi = 0$). Combining the consumption path $r = \rho + g_C$ with $g_\pi = g_Y - g_N$ yields

$$r - g_\pi = \rho + g_N = \rho + n, \tag{15.26}$$

which also uses $g_Y = g_C$. If we define $S_R \equiv L_R/L_Y$, then Equation (15.25) becomes

$$S_R = \frac{1}{1 - \varsigma}\frac{\alpha g_N}{\rho + g_N} = \frac{1}{1 - \varsigma}\frac{\alpha n}{\rho + n}. \tag{15.27}$$

Therefore, the steady-state equilibrium ratio of R&D labour to production labour is increasing in the rate of R&D subsidies as expected.

To equate S_R in (15.27) with S_R^* in (15.18), we need to set the rate of R&D subsidies to the following value:

$$\varsigma^* = 1 - \alpha. \tag{15.28}$$

Given that the capital share is $\alpha \in (1/3, 1/2)$ in the data, our analysis implies that the optimal rate of R&D subsidies can be as high as 50–67%!

15.4. Summary

In this chapter, we derive the socially optimal level of R&D labour in the Jones specification of the Romer model and compare it with the market equilibrium level. We find that the market underinvests in R&D due to the presence of positive R&D externality in the economy. In other words, the model features market failure in the form of R&D underinvestment. In this case, policy intervention by the government subsidising R&D can eliminate the social problem of R&D underinvestment and restore the optimal level of R&D labour in the market equilibrium. However, our model predicts that the required rate of R&D subsidies may be very high.

15.5. Exercises

1. Consider the general law of motion for the number of varieties given by

$$\dot{N}_t = \theta N_t^\phi L_{R,t}. \tag{15.29}$$

   Show that the socially optimal rate of R&D subsidies is given by

$$\varsigma^* = 1 - \alpha \frac{\rho + n}{\rho + n/(1 - \phi)}, \tag{15.30}$$

   which is increasing in ϕ. Intuitively, ϕ is an additional force of R&D externality. When $\phi > 0$, current R&D improves the productivity of future R&D. The productivity of R&D is determined by

$$\frac{\partial \dot{N}_t}{\partial L_{R,t}} = \theta N_t^{\phi}. \tag{15.31}$$

Therefore, when an entrepreneur invests in R&D today, it increases N_t and R&D productivity θN_t^{ϕ} in the future. However, the entrepreneur does not take into account this social benefit of R&D when deciding how much R&D to do. This positive R&D externality is known as intertemporal knowledge spillover.[2]

2. Show that the socially optimal allocation of R&D labour in the Romer model is given by

$$L_R^* = L - \frac{\rho}{\theta}. \tag{15.32}$$

In the Romer model, intertemporal knowledge spillovers are also present because $\dot{N} = \theta N L_R$. Therefore, a larger N leads to a higher R&D productivity θN.

3. Derive the socially optimal rate of R&D subsidies in the Romer model.

---

[2]Jones and Williams (2000) provide a discussion and formalisation of other R&D externalities in the Romer model.

Chapter 16

The Schumpeterian Growth Model

In this chapter, we cover the Schumpeterian quality-ladder model developed by Aghion and Howitt (1992) and follow the treatment of the model in Grossman and Helpman (1991).[1] In the quality-ladder model, economic growth is driven by the development of higher-quality products that replace lower-quality products. Joseph Schumpeter (1942) argues that this process of *creative destruction* is the main engine of long-run economic growth.

As we will show, innovation in the form of quality improvement has a different implication from innovation in the form of new product development.[2] Specifically, the replacement of lower-quality products by higher-quality products gives rise to a business-stealing effect, which is a negative R&D externality. Therefore, in the Schumpeterian growth model, the market economy may exhibit R&D underinvestment or overinvestment, which is different from the Romer model that always exhibits R&D underinvestment.

The Schumpeterian model features the following four components: a representative household; final good; intermediate goods; and R&D. The household supplies labour to the R&D sector and the intermediate-good sector. Then, monopolistic firms that have

---

[1]The materials covered in this chapter are relatively advanced.

[2]Peretto (1994) combines the two dimensions of innovation in quality improvement and new product development to develop the second-generation Schumpeterian growth model that removes the scale effect and endogenises the market structure of the economy.

the most advanced technologies produce differentiated intermediate goods. Finally, a representative final-good firm aggregates intermediate goods into the final good to be consumed by the household.

16.1. Household

There is a representative household which has a log utility function:

$$U = \int_0^\infty e^{-\rho t} \ln C_t dt, \qquad (16.1)$$

where the parameter $\rho > 0$ is the household's discount rate and C_t is the level of consumption at time t. The household maximises utility subject to[3]

$$\dot{F}_t = r_t F_t + W_t L - C_t. \qquad (16.2)$$

r_t is the real interest rate. F_t is the value of financial assets owned by the household. W_t is the wage rate. The household supplies L units of labour. Using Hamiltonian, we can derive the familiar consumption path given by

$$\frac{\dot{C}_t}{C_t} = r_t - \rho. \qquad (16.3)$$

16.2. Final Good

This sector is perfectly competitive, and firms take the output and input prices as given. Final good Y_t is produced by aggregating a unit continuum of differentiated intermediate goods $X_t(i)$ indexed by $i \in [0,1]$. We consider a Cobb–Douglas aggregator given by[4]

$$Y_t = \exp\left(\int_0^1 \ln X_t(i) di\right). \qquad (16.4)$$

---

[3]We do not consider capital in the baseline model and will add capital in an extension.

[4]The aggregator can be re-expressed in a multiplicative form: $Y_t = \Pi_0^1 X_t(i) di$.

From profit maximisation, the demand function for $X_t(i)$ is

$$\frac{\partial Y_t}{\partial X_t(i)} = \frac{Y_t}{X_t(i)} = P_t(i), \tag{16.5}$$

where $P_t(i)$ is the price of $X_t(i)$ for $i \in [0,1]$.

16.3. Intermediate Goods

There is a unit continuum of intermediate goods indexed by $i \in [0,1]$. Each industry i is dominated by a temporary monopolistic leader, who holds a patent on the latest innovation and dominates the market until the next innovation arrives. The production function for the industry leader is

$$X_t(i) = z^{q_t(i)} L_{x,t}(i). \tag{16.6}$$

The parameter $z > 1$ is the step size of a quality improvement. $q_t(i)$ is the number of quality improvements that have occurred in industry i as of time t. In other words, $z^{q_t(i)}$ is the highest level of quality in industry i. $L_{x,t}(i)$ is production labour in industry i.

The industry leader's marginal cost of producing $X_t(i)$ is

$$MC_t(i) = \frac{W_t}{z^{q_t(i)}}. \tag{16.7}$$

To derive the equilibrium price, we assume that the current and former industry leaders engage in Bertrand competition. Because the current industry leader's product has a higher quality by a factor of z, the profit-maximising price for the current leader is a constant markup over the marginal cost.

$$P_t(i) = \mu MC_t(i), \tag{16.8}$$

where the markup ratio $\mu \in (1, z]$ is less than or equal to the quality step size, depending on the level of patent protection, which determines the market power of the industry leader.[5] Monopolistic profit

---

[5]Aghion and Howitt (1992) and Grossman and Helpman (1991) assume that the markup ratio is determined by the quality step size z. Li (2001) generalises the Schumpeterian model by introducing a patent policy parameter $\mu \leq z$ that determines the markup ratio.

in industry i is

$$\pi_t(i) = [P_t(i) - MC_t(i)] X_t(i)$$
$$= \left(\frac{\mu - 1}{\mu}\right) P_t(i) X_t(i) = \left(\frac{\mu - 1}{\mu}\right) Y_t, \qquad (16.9)$$

where the last equality uses (16.5) and (16.8). Finally, wage income to production labour is

$$W_t L_{x,t}(i) = MC_t(i) X_t(i) = \frac{P_t(i) X_t(i)}{\mu} = \frac{Y_t}{\mu}. \qquad (16.10)$$

16.4.   R&D

Denote the value of an invention in industry i as $v_t(i)$. Due to the Cobb–Douglas specification in (16.4), the amount of profit is the same across industries (i.e., $\pi_t(i) = \pi_t$ for $i \in [0, 1]$). As a result, $v_t(i) = v_t$ in a symmetric equilibrium in which the arrival rate of innovation is equal across industries.[6] The value of an invention is given by

$$v_t = \frac{\pi_t}{r - g_\pi + \sigma}. \qquad (16.11)$$

The present value of monopolistic profits is discounted by $r - g_\pi + \sigma$, where σ is the arrival rate of innovation, because when an innovation arrives, the current industry leader loses the market to the next industry leader.

Competitive R&D entrepreneurs hire R&D labour $L_{r,t}$ to create inventions. The expected benefit of R&D is $v_t \sigma_t$ whereas the cost of R&D is $W_t L_{r,t}$. Zero expected profit in R&D implies that

$$v_t \sigma_t = W_t L_{r,t}. \qquad (16.12)$$

---

[6]Cozzi *et al.* (2007) provide a theoretical foundation for the symmetric equilibrium to be the unique rational-expectation equilibrium in the Schumpeterian model.

The arrival rate of innovation is $\sigma_t = \theta L_{r,t}$, where the parameter $\theta > 0$ determines R&D productivity. Therefore, (16.12) can be re-expressed as

$$\theta v_t = W_t. \tag{16.13}$$

This R&D condition determines the allocation of labour between production and R&D.

16.5. Aggregation

Substituting (16.6) into (16.4) yields the aggregate production function:

$$Y_t = A_t L_{x,t}, \tag{16.14}$$

where the (log) level of aggregate technology A_t is defined as

$$\ln A_t \equiv \left(\int_0^1 q_t(i)di \right) \ln z = \left(\int_0^t \sigma_s ds \right) \ln z. \tag{16.15}$$

The last equality uses the law of large numbers, which equates the average number of quality improvements $\int_0^1 q_t(i)di$ that have occurred as of time t to the total number of innovation arrivals $\int_0^t \sigma_s ds$ up to time t. Differentiating $\ln A_t$ with respect to time yields the law of motion for A_t given by[7]

$$\frac{\dot{A}_t}{A_t} = \sigma_t \ln z. \tag{16.16}$$

Therefore, the steady-state growth rate of technology is $g_A = \sigma \ln z = (\theta \ln z) L_r$, which is increasing in R&D labour L_r.

16.6. Market Equilibrium Level of R&D

In this model without capital, all the final good is consumed by the household such that

$$Y_t = C_t. \tag{16.17}$$

---

[7]Here, we apply the Leibniz rule for differentiation under the integral sign.

Also, the labour market must clear such that

$$L_{x,t} + L_{r,t} = L. \tag{16.18}$$

To solve for the steady-state equilibrium labour allocation, we use

$$g_\pi = g_Y = g_C, \tag{16.19}$$

where g_π denotes the growth rate of the profit in (16.9). Substituting (16.9), (16.10), (16.11) and (16.19) into the R&D condition in (16.13) yields

$$\theta(\mu - 1)L_x = \theta L_r + \rho, \tag{16.20}$$

where $r - g_\pi = \rho$ because $g_\pi = g_Y = g_C$. Combining (16.18) and (16.20) yields the market equilibrium level of R&D labour given by

$$L_r(\underset{-}{\rho}, \underset{+}{\theta}, \underset{+}{\mu}, \underset{+}{L}) = \left(\frac{\mu - 1}{\mu}\right) L - \frac{\rho}{\mu\theta}. \tag{16.21}$$

The comparative statics are as follows. L_r is decreasing in ρ because a higher discount rate decreases the present value of future monopolistic profits. L_r is increasing in θ because higher R&D productivity increases the incentives for R&D. L_r is increasing in μ because a larger markup increases the amount of monopolistic profit, which determines the private return to R&D. Finally, L_r is increasing in L implying the presence of the scale effect.[8]

16.7. Socially Optimal Level of R&D

In this section, we derive the socially optimal allocation of the model. Suppose a benevolent social planner maximises the household's utility $U = \int_0^\infty e^{-\rho t} \ln C_t dt$ subject to the aggregate production $C_t = A_t L_{x,t}$, the law of motion for technology $\dot{A}_t = A_t(\theta \ln z)L_{r,t}$ and the labour resource constraint $L_{x,t} + L_{r,t} = L$. Then, setting up

---

[8]See Segerstrom (1998) for a semi-endogenous-growth version of the Schumpeterian model.

the Hamiltonian function

$$H_t = \ln A_t + \ln(L - L_{r,t}) + \lambda_t A_t (\theta \ln z) L_{r,t},$$

we can derive the optimal allocation of R&D labour L_r^* given by[9]

$$L_r^*(\underset{-}{\rho}, \underset{+}{\theta}, \underset{+}{z}, \underset{+}{L}) = L - \frac{\rho}{\theta \ln z}. \tag{16.22}$$

Comparing (16.21) and (16.22), we see that the market equilibrium allocation L_r is not necessarily equal to and can be larger or smaller than the socially optimal allocation L_r^*. Specifically, there exists a threshold value of the markup ratio μ above (below) which the market equilibrium allocation L_r is above (below) the socially optimal allocation L_r^*. The threshold $\overline{\mu}$ is

$$\overline{\mu} \equiv \left(1 + \frac{\theta L}{\rho}\right) \ln z,$$

which is increasing in the quality step size z.

The reason is that the Schumpeterian growth model features both positive and negative externalities of R&D. Intertemporal knowledge spillover in $\dot{A}_t = A_t(\theta \ln z) L_{r,t}$ is a positive externality of R&D, whereas the business-stealing effect (i.e., new industry leaders taking over the market from current industry leaders) is a negative externality of R&D. It is useful to note that this business-stealing effect is absent in the Romer model, which features only positive externality. When the positive externality dominates the negative externality, the market underinvests in R&D such that $L_r < L_r^*$. R&D underinvestment happens when the quality step size z, which captures the social benefit of R&D, is sufficiently large. When the negative externality dominates the positive externality, the market overinvests in R&D such that $L_r > L_r^*$. R&D overinvestment happens when the markup μ, which captures the private benefit of R&D, is sufficiently large.

16.8. Capital

The canonical quality-ladder model does not feature physical capital K_t. In this section, we extend the quality-ladder model by allowing

---

[9]The derivations of L_r^* are left as an exercise.

for capital accumulation. We assume for simplicity that only the intermediate-good sector employs capital. We modify the production function (16.6) to

$$X_t(i) = z^{q_t(i)}[K_t(i)]^\alpha [L_{x,t}(i)]^{1-\alpha}, \tag{16.23}$$

where the parameter $\alpha \in (0,1)$ determines the intensity of capital $K_t(i)$ in the production of $X_t(i)$. From cost minimisation, the marginal cost of production is

$$MC_t(i) = \frac{1}{z^{q_t(i)}} \left(\frac{R_t}{\alpha}\right)^\alpha \left(\frac{W_t}{1-\alpha}\right)^{1-\alpha}, \tag{16.24}$$

where R_t denotes the rental price of capital. The profit income is still given by (16.9) whereas capital income and production-labour income are, respectively,

$$R_t K_t = \frac{\alpha Y_t}{\mu}, \tag{16.25}$$

$$W_t L_{x,t} = \frac{(1-\alpha)Y_t}{\mu}. \tag{16.26}$$

Substituting (16.9), (16.19) and (16.26) into (16.13) yields

$$\theta(\mu - 1)L_x = (1 - \alpha)(\theta L_r + \rho). \tag{16.27}$$

Combining (16.18) and (16.27) yields the market equilibrium level of R&D labour given by

$$L_r(\rho, \theta, \mu, L, \alpha) = \left(\frac{\mu - 1}{\mu - \alpha}\right) L - \left(\frac{1-\alpha}{\mu - \alpha}\right) \frac{\rho}{\theta}. \tag{16.28}$$
$${\scriptstyle -\ +\ +\ +\ +}$$

The comparative statics for ρ, θ, μ and L are the same as before. As for the capital intensity, L_r is increasing in α because a decrease in labour intensity in production reduces the usage of labour for production and leads to more labour available for R&D.

To complete the analysis in this section, we substitute (16.23) into (16.4) to derive the aggregate production given by

$$Y_t = A_t K_t^\alpha L_{x,t}^{1-\alpha}. \tag{16.29}$$

Also, the resource constraint on the final good is

$$Y_t = C_t + I_t, \tag{16.30}$$

and the law of motion for capital accumulation is

$$\dot{K}_t = I_t - \delta K_t. \tag{16.31}$$

Along the balanced-growth path, the growth rate of output equals the growth rate of capital; therefore, the long-run growth rate of output is

$$g_Y = \left(\frac{1}{1-\alpha}\right) g_A = \left(\frac{\theta \ln z}{1-\alpha}\right) L_r, \tag{16.32}$$

where the market equilibrium level of L_r has been derived in (16.28).

16.9. Summary

In this chapter, we develop the Schumpeterian growth model in which innovation is driven by the quality improvement of existing products, instead of the development of new products as in the Romer model. In addition to the usual positive R&D externality, this alternative engine of innovation gives rise to negative R&D externality in the form of a business-stealing effect, in which entrants take away the market share of incumbents when inventing a higher-quality product. As a result of this negative R&D externality, the market may overinvest or underinvest in R&D. R&D overinvestment occurs when firms have too much market power which determines the private benefit of R&D, whereas R&D underinvestment occurs given a sufficiently large quality step size which determines the social benefit of R&D.

16.10. Exercises

1. Consider the Schumpeterian growth model without capital. Use the Hamiltonian function

$$H_t = \ln A_t + \ln(L - L_{r,t}) + \lambda_t A_t (\theta \ln z) L_{r,t}, \tag{16.33}$$

to show that the optimal allocation of R&D labour L_r^* is given by

$$L_r^* = L - \frac{\rho}{\theta \ln z}. \tag{16.34}$$

2. Suppose the government provides R&D subsidies. Derive the equilibrium level of R&D labour in the Schumpeterian growth model without capital.

3. Consider the introduction of leisure to the household's utility function:

$$U = \int_0^\infty e^{-\rho t}[\ln C_t + \beta \ln(L - l_t)]dt, \qquad (16.35)$$

where the parameter $\beta > 0$ determines the importance of leisure $L - l_t$ in the utility function. In this case, the asset-accumulation becomes

$$\dot{F}_t = r_t F_t + W_t l_t - C_t. \qquad (16.36)$$

Show that the equilibrium level of R&D labour in the Schumpeterian growth model without capital is given by

$$L_r = \frac{1}{1+\beta}\left[\left(\frac{\mu - 1}{\mu}\right)L - (1 + \beta\mu)\frac{\rho}{\mu\theta}\right], \qquad (16.37)$$

which is the same as (16.21) when $\beta = 0$.

4. Suppose the price regulation policy is not binding, i.e., $\mu \geq z$. In this case, the Bertrand competition between the current and former industry leaders implies

$$P_t(i) = zMC_t(i). \qquad (16.38)$$

Derive the equilibrium level of R&D labour L_r and the growth rate of output.

Chapter 17

Appendix on Dynamic Optimisation

In this appendix, we demonstrate how to use a mathematical tool known as the Hamiltonian (named after William Rowan Hamilton) to solve dynamic optimisation problems in continuous time. We use the Ramsey model as an example. The household's lifetime utility function is given by

$$U = \int_0^\infty e^{-\rho t} u(C_t) dt, \tag{17.1}$$

where $u(C_t)$ is a differentiable, strictly increasing and concave function in C_t,[1] which denotes consumption. The parameter $\rho > 0$ is the subjective discount rate. The household maximises utility in (17.1) subject to the following capital-accumulation equation:

$$\dot{K}_t = F(K_t) - C_t, \tag{17.2}$$

where $\dot{K}_t \equiv \partial K_t / \partial t$ denotes the change in the level of capital with respect to time t, and $F(K_t)$ is a differentiable and concave production function in K_t net of capital depreciation.[2]

---

[1] In the main text, we consider a log utility function $u(C_t) = \ln C_t$ for simplicity.

[2] In the main text, we consider a Cobb–Douglas production function for simplicity.

The household maximises (17.1) subject to (17.2). To solve this dynamic optimisation problem, we use the Hamiltonian. The current-value Hamiltonian function H_t is given by[3]

$$H_t = u(C_t) + \lambda_t[F(K_t) - C_t]. \tag{17.3}$$

In other words, the Hamiltonian function at time t consists of (a) the utility function $u(C_t)$, (b) the right-hand side of the capital-accumulation equation $F(K_t) - C_t$, and (c) a multiplier λ_t (known as the co-state variable) for the capital-accumulation equation. To maximise the household's utility, we derive the first-order conditions with respect to $\{C_t, K_t, \lambda_t\}$:

$$\frac{\partial H_t}{\partial C_t} = \frac{\partial u(C_t)}{\partial C_t} - \lambda_t = 0, \tag{17.4}$$

$$\frac{\partial H_t}{\partial K_t} = \lambda_t \frac{\partial F(K_t)}{\partial K_t} = \lambda_t \rho - \dot{\lambda}_t, \tag{17.5}$$

$$\frac{\partial H_t}{\partial \lambda_t} = F(K_t) - C_t = \dot{K}_t. \tag{17.6}$$

It is useful to note that K_t is a state variable (i.e., a variable that accumulates over time),[4] so we have to treat its first-order condition differently. Instead of equating $\partial H_t/\partial K_t$ to zero, we set $\partial H_t/\partial K_t = \lambda_t \rho - \dot{\lambda}_t$. As for the first-order condition with respect to the co-state variable λ_t, it simply yields the capital-accumulation in (17.2). If the household is maximising utility in (17.1), then its consumption behaviour and its accumulation of capital must satisfy (17.4)–(17.6).

Suppose $u(C_t) = \ln C_t$. Then, (17.4) can be expressed as

$$\lambda_t = \frac{\partial u(C_t)}{\partial C_t} = \frac{1}{C_t}, \tag{17.7}$$

where $1/C_t$ is the marginal utility of consumption. Taking the log of (17.7) yields

$$\ln \lambda_t = -\ln C_t. \tag{17.8}$$

---

[3]There is an alternative formulation, known as the present-value Hamiltonian.
[4]In contrast, C_t is a control variable that can jump to a different value at any time t.

Differentiating both sides of (17.8) with respect to t yields[5]

$$\frac{\dot{\lambda}_t}{\lambda_t} = -\frac{\dot{C}_t}{C_t}.$$ (17.9)

Substituting (17.9) into (17.5) yields

$$\frac{\dot{C}_t}{C_t} = -\frac{\dot{\lambda}_t}{\lambda_t} = \frac{\partial F(K_t)}{\partial K_t} - \rho,$$ (17.10)

where $\partial F(K_t)/\partial K_t$ is the marginal product of capital net of depreciation. $\dot{C}_t/C_t$ in (17.10) is the optimal consumption path of the household. If the household is maximising utility, then its evolution of consumption must satisfy the optimal consumption path in (17.10). Also, its accumulation of capital must satisfy the capital-accumulation equation in (17.2). Finally, one can use (17.2) and (17.10) to draw a two-dimension phase diagram to show that C_t and K_t converge to a steady state with $\dot{C}_t = \dot{K}_t = 0$.[6]

---

[5]Note that $\frac{\partial \ln \lambda_t}{\partial t} = \frac{1}{\lambda_t} \frac{\partial \lambda_t}{\partial t} = \frac{\dot{\lambda}_t}{\lambda_t}$.

[6]See Romer (2018, Chapter 2).

References

1. Acemoglu, D., 2009. *Introduction to Modern Economic Growth*. Princeton, NJ: Princeton University Press.
2. Aghion, P., and Howitt, P., 1992. A model of growth through creative destruction. *Econometrica*, 60, 323–351.
3. Aghion, P., and Howitt, P., 2009. *The Economics of Growth*. Cambridge, MA: MIT Press.
4. Barro, R., 1974. Are government bonds net wealth? *Journal of Political Economy*, 82, 1095–1117.
5. Barro, R., Chu, A., and Cozzi., G., 2017. *Intermediate Macroeconomics*. Cengage Learning.
6. Barro, R., and Redlick, C., 2011. Macroeconomic effects from government purchases and taxes. *Quarterly Journal of Economics*, 126, 51–102.
7. Barro, R., and Sala-i-Martin, X., 2003. *Economic Growth*. Cambridge, MA: MIT Press.
8. Baxter, M., and King, R., 1993. Fiscal policy in general equilibrium. *American Economic Review*, 83, 315–334.
9. Cass, D., 1965. Optimum growth in an aggregative model of capital accumulation. *Review of Economic Studies*, 32, 233–240.
10. Chu, A., 2018. From Solow to Romer: Teaching endogenous technological change in undergraduate economics. *International Review of Economics Education*, 27, 10–15.
11. Cozzi, G., 2017a. Endogenous growth, semi-endogenous growth. . . or both? A simple hybrid model. *Economics Letters*, 154, 28–30.
12. Cozzi, G., 2017b. Combining semi-endogenous and fully endogenous growth: A generalization. *Economics Letters*, 155, 89–91.
13. Cozzi, G., Giordani, P., and Zamparelli, L., 2007. The refoundation of the symmetric equilibrium in Schumpeterian growth models. *Journal of Economic Theory*, 136, 788–797.
14. Dixit, A., and Stiglitz, J., 1977. Monopolistic competition and optimum product diversity. *American Economic Review*, 67, 297–308.

15.   Gali, J., 2015. *Monetary Policy, Inflation, and the Business Cycle: An Intro-duction to the New Keynesian Framework and its Applications*. Princeton, NJ: Princeton University Press.

16.   Galor, O., 2011. *Unified Growth Theory*. Princeton, NJ: Princeton University Press.

17.   Grossman, G., and Helpman, E., 1991. Quality ladders in the theory of growth. *Review of Economic Studies*, 58, 43–61.

18.   Jones, C., 1995. R&D-based models of economic growth. *Journal of Political Economy*, 103, 759–784.

19.   Jones, C., and Vollrath, D., 2013. *Introduction to Economic Growth*. New York: W. W. Norton & Company.

20.   Jones, C., and Williams, J., 2000. Too much of a good thing? The economics of investment in R&D. *Journal of Economic Growth*, 5, 65–85.

21.   Kimball, M., 1995. The quantitative analytics of the basic neomonetarist model. *Journal of Money, Credit and Banking*, 27, 1241–1277.

22.   Koopmans, T., 1965. On the concept of optimal economic growth. In: *The Econometric Approach to Development Planning*, Amsterdam: North-Holland Publishing Company.

23.   Kydland, F. and Prescott, E., 1982. Time to build and aggregate fluctua-tions. *Econometrica*, 50, 1345–1370.

24.   Li, C.-W., 2001. On the policy implications of endogenous technological progress. *Economic Journal*, 111, C164–C179.

25.   McCandless, G., 2008. *ABCs of RBCs: An Introduction to Dynamic Macroe-conomic Models*. Cambridge, MA: Harvard University Press.

26.   Peretto, P., 1994. *Essays on Market Structure and Economic Growth*. Ph.D. dissertation, Yale University.

27.   Ramsey, F., 1928. A mathematical theory of saving. *Economic Journal*, 38, 543–559.

28.   Romer, D., 2018. *Advanced Macroeconomics*. New York: McGraw-Hill Education.

29.   Romer, P., 1990. Endogenous technological change. *Journal of Political Economy*, 98, S71–S102.

30.   Schumpeter, J., 1942. *Capitalism, Socialism and Democracy*. New York: Harper and Brothers.

31.   Segerstrom, P., 1998. Endogenous growth without scale effects. *American Economic Review*, 88, 1290–1310.

32.   Solow, R., 1956. A contribution to the theory of economic growth. *Quarterly Journal of Economics*, 70, 65–94.

33.   Swan, T., 1956. Economic growth and capital accumulation. *Economic Record*, 32, 334–361.

Index

Printed in the United States
by Baker & Taylor Publisher Services